UFOS AND SECRET SOCIETIES

BY

KEN HUDNALL

OMEGA PRESS
EL PASO, TEXAS

UFOS AND SECRET SOCIETIES
COPYRIGHT © 2012 KEN HUDNALL

All rights reserved. No part of this book may be reproduced or transmitted in any form or by any means, graphic, electronic, or mechanical, including photocopying, recording, taping or by any information storage or retrieval system, without the permission in writing from the publisher.

OMEGA PRESS
An imprint of Omega Communications Group, Inc.

For information contact:
Omega Press
5823 N. Mesa, #839
El Paso, Texas 79912

Or http://www.kenhudnall.com

FIRST EDITION

Printed in the United States of America

OTHER WORKS BY THE SAME AUTHOR UNDER THE NAME KEN HUDNALL FROM OMEGA PRESS

MANHATTAN CONSPIRACY SERIES
Blood on the Apple
Capitol Crimes
Angel of Death

THE OCCULT CONNECTION
UFOs, Secret Societies and Ancient Gods
The Hidden Race

DARKNESS
When Darkness Falls
Fear The Darkness

SPIRITS OF THE BORDER
(with Connie Wang)
The History and Mystery of El Paso Del Norte
The History and Mystery of Fort Bliss, Texas

(with Sharon Hudnall)
The History and Mystery of the Rio Grande
The History and Mystery of New Mexico
The History and Mystery of the Lone Star State
The History and Mystery of Arizona
The History and Mystery of Tombstone, AZ
The History and Mystery of Colorado
Echoes of the Past
El Paso: A City of Secrets
Tales From The Nightshift

THE ESTATE SALE MURDERS
Dead Man's Diary

Northwood Conspiracy

No Safe Haven; Homeland Insecurity

Where No Car Has Gone Before

Seventy Years and No Losses: The History of the Sun Bowl

How Not To Get Published

PUBLISHED BY PAJA BOOKS
The Occult Connection: Unidentified Flying Objects

DEDICATION

As with all of my books, I could not have completed this book if not for my lovely wife, Sharon.

TABLE OF CONTENTS

Contents
- SECRET SOCIETIES 11
- IN THE BEGINNING 17
- CONSPIRACIES 21
- MEN IN BLACK 31
- NON-HUMANS AMONG US 45
- UNITED STATES SECRETS 61
- MEN OF DISTINCTION 69
- DE'JA'VU ALL OVER AGAIN 87
- SHADOW PEOPLE FOR A SHADOW WORLD 101
- ANCIENT ORDERS 109
- AGENTS OF THE UNSEEN 129
- MODERN VERSION OF AN OLD PROGRAM 139
- MOTHER OF ALL SECRET SOCIETIES 149
- THE MASTERS 163
- THE WRAP-UP 199
- INDEX 201

CHAPTER ONE
SECRET SOCIETIES

Figure 1: Secret orders

The appellation secret society is a term used to describe certain clubs or organizations in which the activities and inner functioning of those societies are concealed from non-members[1]. This hidden organization or secret society may or may not attempt to conceal its very existence from the world. The term usually excludes covert groups, such as intelligence agencies or guerrilla groups, which hide their activities and memberships but still maintain a public presence and in fact may well be funded by public funds.

The exact qualifications for labeling a group as a secret society are disputed, but definitions generally rely on the degree to which the organization insists on secrecy, and might also involve the supposed retention and transmission of secret knowledge, denial of membership in or knowledge of the group, the creation of personal bonds between

---

[1]Wikipedia

members of the organization, and the use of secret rites or rituals which solidify members of the group.

Alan Axelrod, author of the *International Encyclopedia of Secret Societies and Fraternal Orders*[2], defines a secret society as an organization that is exclusive, claims to own or be charged with protecting special secrets and shows a strong inclination to favor its own members over non-members in such things as hiring. David V. Barrett, author of *Secret Societies: From the Ancient and Arcane to the Modern and Clandestine*[3], uses slightly different terms to define what, in his opinion, does and does not qualify as a secret society. He defines it as any group that possesses the following characteristics:

- It has "carefully graded and progressed teachings"
- These teachings are "available only to selected individuals"
- The teachings lead to "hidden (and 'unique') truths"
- Truths bring "personal benefits beyond the reach and even the understanding of the uninitiated.

Whatever may be the definition of secret societies one thing is certain; many of the world's elite are members of one of more organizations that would be considered a secret society. The question of precisely what fires the will of the wealthy supranational elites seeking to manipulate and control world events, has not escaped the attention of serious students of conspiracies and cover-ups. There are many who believe that there is one deeply hidden major secret society that gives birth to others all of which work to one end, world domination. The question is what keeps the conspiracy moving forward over so many eons?

The late American Professor Revilo P. Oliver[4], a confirmed atheist, was forced to conclude: "*A theory that a conspiracy has been*

---

[2]Axelrod, Alan, International Encyclopedia of Secret Societies and Fraternal Orders, Checkmark Books (August 1998)
[3]Barrett, David V., Secret Societies: From the Ancient and Arcane to the Modern and Clandestine, Blandford Pr (April 1999).
[4]Revilo Pendleton Oliver (July 7, 1908 — August 20, 1994) was an American professor of Classical philology, Spanish, and Italian at the University of Illinois at Urbana-Champaign, who wrote and polemicized extensively for white nationalist causes.

working consciously for many centuries is not very plausible unless one attributes to them a religious unity. That is tantamount to regarding them as Satanists engaged in the worship and service of supernatural evil.

The directors of the conspiracy must see or otherwise directly perceive manifestations which convince them of the existence and power of Lucifer. And since subtle conspirators must be very shrewd men, not likely to be deceived by auto-suggestion, hypnosis, or drugs, we should have to conclude that they probably are in contact with a force of pure evil[5]."

So there is a certain religious manifestation to any long lived conspiracy. This certainly fits in with the theory that this book will present. Now it is not being maintained that there is an organized religion behind the secret societies that will be discussed, but it will be shown that there is actually a form of religious frenzy that fuels many of these hidden organizations. This religious underpinning, this author would submit, comes from the fact that those who started the original secret societies were actually those that we referred to in history and the gods. Gods who were actually

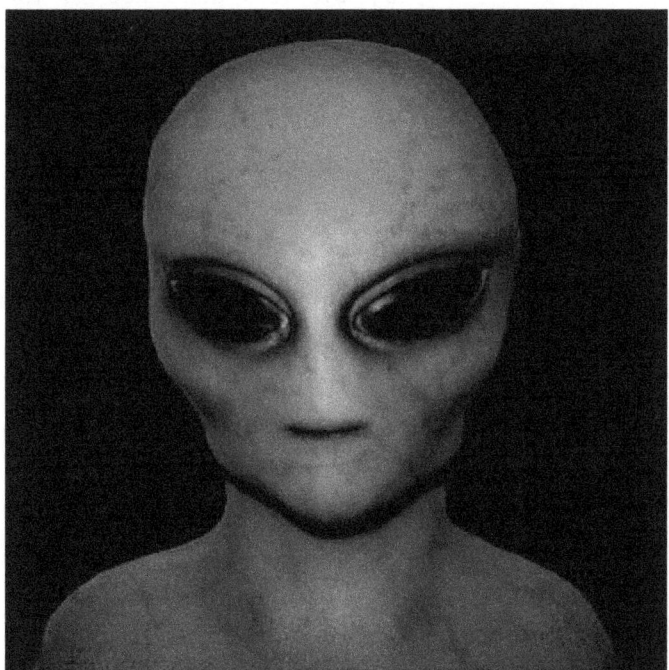

Figure 2: Alien Figure

---

[5]Oliver, Revilo P. Rev., Conspiracy or Degeneracy?,

visitors to this planet and both the creators as well as the enslavers of the human race.

As laid out in *The Occult Connection: Unidentified Flying Objects*[6] it is this author's opinion that this planet has long been visited by one or more advanced races. Add to this eons long visitation by more advanced species the effects of what we have come to known as Clark's Law and you have a situation ripe for the creation of a new religion complete with its own gods. Oh, for those of you not familiar with Clark's Law[7], it states that *"any sufficiently advanced technology is indistinguishable from magic"*.

Entities able to perform such miracles have long been worshipped by the less advanced or the less educated down through history. A prime example of the result of a primitive culture becoming associated with a more advanced culture is found in the various cargo cults that sprang up during World War II. A cargo cult is a type of religious practice that may appear in traditional tribal societies in the wake of interaction with technologically advanced cultures. The cults are focused on obtaining the material wealth (the "cargo") of the advanced culture through magic and religious rituals and practices, believing that the wealth was intended for them by their deities and ancestors. Cargo cults developed primarily in remote parts of New Guinea and other Melanesian and Micronesian societies in the southwest Pacific Ocean, beginning with the first significant arrivals of Westerners in the 19th century. Similar behaviors have, however, also appeared elsewhere in the world[8].

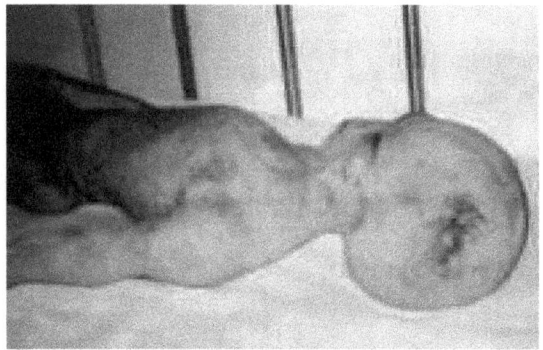

Figure 3: Alien Body

---

[6]Hudnall, Ken, The Occult Connection: Unidentified Flying Objects, Paja Books, Pittsburgh, PA, 2009.
[7]Clark's Law was promulgated by Arthur C. Clark, author and scientist.
[8]Wikipedia

Cargo cult activity in the Pacific region increased significantly during and immediately after World War II, when large amounts of manpower and materials were brought in by both the Japanese as well as American combatants, and this was observed by the residents of these regions. As transport planes crashed, as happens in war time, cult members came into possession of "goods". When the war ended, the military bases were closed and the flow of goods and materials available to the natives ceased. In an attempt to attract further deliveries of goods, followers of the cults engaged in ritualistic practices such as building crude imitation landing strips, aircraft and radio equipment, and mimicking the behavior that they had observed of the military personnel operating them.

This certainly parallels some of the legends that have come down to us from ancient times regarding such things as Rama and his flying ship from the Rig Veda[9]. To those of the Cargo Cult, those who flew overhead (the various air forces) were gods who could dispense wealth and favors as they desired. A religion grew up around the "mana from the skies." Is it any different than how our distant ancestors viewed

Figure 4: Ancient gods or aliens?

---

[9] The Rig Veda is an ancient Indian sacred collection of Vedic Sanskrit hymns. It is counted among the four canonical sacred texts (śruti) of Hinduism known as the Vedas.

those that dispensed wealth to them. Are not prayers and other religious ceremonies ritualistic practices indulged in by the believers to try and entice deliveries of "goods" from the gods or God? Think about it.

The interesting thing about those who appear to be either directly or indirectly associated with the gods of antiquity, it would appear that they have a very long running plan that seems to be coming close to fruition. This plan seems to involve pruning the herd so to speak. But more on that later.

But in every group there is one or two who know the truth behind the myths and legends. It is these individuals who use that knowledge to profit from the awe of the rest of the group. It is those few who form the inner core of what we would call a secret society and, I believe, may have been members of the ultimate secret society. We are left with question after question. And thus it begins.

CHAPTER TWO

IN THE BEGINNING

In 1989, the author published *The Occult Connection: UFOs, Secret Societies and Ancient Gods*[10]. In this work, a new theory was outlined that the entities that were discussed in that volume who were (and are) behind the UFOs worked through secret societies and the ancient gods of history to guide and subvert the human race from its very beginning. Since that time, there has been an unbelievable shift in the direction of not only this country but the world political structure as a whole. Was it just coincidence that we as a people have moved closer to centralized government as it was practiced thousands of years ago or was it a part of an overall plan? From history we find the answer. From history we find that we are being herded toward a defined end just like a herd of cattle is led to the slaughter. We are the victims, but who are the masters?

Figure 5: An unidentified flying object

---

[10] Hudnall, Ken, The Occult Connection: UFOs, Secret Societies and Ancient Gods, Omega Press, Anaheim, California, 1989.

In fact, an unbiased reading of history makes it clear that there is little doubt that the Human Race has long been guided from behind the scenes; the questions are who, or what, is doing the guiding and why they have taken such an interest in the development of the Human race? In spite of the assurance made by the author above there is little direct evidence of the existence of these "guides", but there is certainly a great deal of circumstantial evidence that they are real and have always been with us.

Most people, if they even think about it, assume that the UFO phenomena started about forty years ago when UFOs started being widely observed and reported by people in all walks of life. Unfortunately, there was little real investigation done into these strange lights in the sky as most newspapers considered UFOs as things to be reported only when there was no "real" news. However, in 1947 pilot Kenneth Arnold sighted flying silver disks near Mount Rainer and that same year the Roswell crash took place. These two events got the attention of the world.

A review of history shows that UFOs have traveled our skies long before 1947. Actually, UFOs have sailed our skies since before the

Figure 6: Cave drawing

beginning of recorded history. There are drawings on the walls of caves dating back thousands upon thousands of years depicting similar aerial craft flying in those ancient skies. Every ancient civilization of which we have records talks about the "gods" coming down, in flying vehicles I might point out, and walking among man. There are numerous writings about some of the ancient Gods actually leading human armies and engaging in hand to hand combat with their enemies. A literal reading of the earliest of man's written records, from the Sumerian Civilization, makes it appear that the "gods" of early man were actual beings who lived and loved, fought and could be killed, just like man[11]. Assuming that this might be true, it is, perhaps, not surprising that these "gods" used recognizable technology and made use of flying aids that we can recognize today, such as the well-known silver disks.

The discovery that our accounts of ancient Gods might actually be accounts of living beings was nothing new. The ancient records have been available to us for a number of years, some since the late 1800's, others, such as the Holy Bible, for close to two thousand years. What began to make the stories be examined closely for their validity were the discoveries that each was based on an earlier writing by an older civilization. Eventually, this inter-connecting chain of relationships led back to the first human civilization, that of ancient Samaria.

However, modern science refused to credit the fact that civilizations

Figure 7: Sky Chariot

before us might have been as advanced, or even more so, than are we today. So stories of "gods" flying in "sky chariots" and using recognizable

---

11 Sitchin, Zecharia, THE 12TH PLANET, Avon Books, New York. 1976.

technology to work "miracles" were, and are, dismissed as folk tales. (I would point out that some of the technology that we use today would be considered magic to people living a hundred years ago.)

If these old stories are actually just folk tales, then all of these tales are ancient science fiction. Our forefathers must have spent a great deal of time dreaming up stories and then proceeded to spread them throughout the ancient world.

Scientists of our civilization, thinking that our technology is the most advanced in the history of this planet, have been hard pressed to deal with the ancient reports that we have been examined and studied by a race or races far in advance of our own. Science requires that things be replicable in the lab. As a result most of these so-called research scientists look for some concrete proof, such as a signed confession of one of the aliens, to prove that there may have been such contact eons ago.

A lot of data that has been gathered by civilian researchers points to aspects of this phenomenon that while they would prove the validity of the old records, are simply too far out to be accepted by mainstream America. The usual response given by the layman to a question regarding the reality of UFOs is usually something similar to, "If all of this is true, why hasn't the government either told us about it or done something about it?" This is a most interesting question, one that we will try to answer as we progress through this book.

CHAPTER TWO
CONSPIRACIES

Now, it is necessary at this point to ask for a certain amount of patience and understanding by the readers. In our examination of secret societies we must first look into the relationship between UFOs and certain ancient secret societies. Circumstantially, there is a tremendous body of data that holds that the gods fly in our skies, overseeing their creations. Support for this premise is found in almost every religion in the world.

Among UFO researchers, there is no secret that much information, as well as hard evidence of the reality of the UFO phenomena, has been suppressed both by civilian researchers and by our own Government as well. I am sorry to say that some of the most blatant suppression has actually not been by our Government, but instead as a result of civilian researcher "ego" trips, where one researcher attempts to "own" certain data that should be public domain.

As a result of the suppression and, apparent compartmentalization of other information, the average member of our civilization is, at one and the same time both denied important information and bombarded with conflicting reports of the reality of incidents. Part of our population either does not or will not believe in the existence of possible "little men from outer space". Most point to alleged scientific findings that make such a thing impossible. Other, more inquisitive members of our population, acknowledges the existence of other species or at least the probability of their existence. It is to this part of our population that I direct this book.

AN INVESTIGATIVE NIGHTMARE

Investigations into most topics of the paranormal usually results in a tremendous amount of conflicting findings. The research into the UFO mystery seems to follow a similar course. Those who believe that the UFOs are piloted by entities from outer space, tend to find evidence to support this contention. From eyewitness accounts to landing traces, there is usually so much evidence found to support this contention that it is hard to see where others get the idea that it is all a hoax. However, at the same time, those who do feel that it is all a hoax, can dig around at the alleged landing site and usually find proof that the whole thing was a hoax, usually carried out either by teenagers or publicity seekers, such as the two painters who claim to be responsible for creating every crop circle in the world. Then there is the third group who always feels that a UFO sighting is merely a misidentification of a natural event. There are always claims that they have found some natural happening that could, with a great stretch of the imagination, be mistaken for a landing spaceship. So what are we to believe?

As I have outlined in earlier works, my belief is that we are dealing with a phenomenon that tries to be all things to all people. I believe that it is intentionally misleading researchers in order to protect its' own identity and to limit outside interference in its activities. It takes on many forms in order to deal with many types of people. To those who are fanatically religious, it assumes the cloak of an Angel or a Demon. To those who are prone to believe in life in outer space, it takes on the appearance of a spaceman. But beneath it all, I feel lies an earthbound entity who is fighting for its' own survival. As we progress through this book, I will give my reasons for this belief.

In order to deal with the information that I will present and internalize it in such a way that you can begin to understand my theory you will need to suspend your credulity. This subject is so unbelievable that this very fact that it is unbelievable can, and has, acted as a shield for this Entity.

For centuries, this force or intelligence, or whatever you want to call it has been leading us down the garden path. It is true, I believe, that this is an Alien Presence, but I find evidence that it has been here for so long that it is actually more earthling that we are, but more on this point as we go along.

PAWNS OF THE GODS

Figure 8: Gods of Egypt

This mysterious Presence has used and abused us since before the beginning of recorded history. There is evidence that this Presence has used us as pawns in wars of both attrition and conquest. To it, or them, we are expendable, about as valuable as lab rats. As long as what we want corresponds with what it, or they want, everything is fine. In such a case, they are "Benevolent". It is these "Benevolent Ones" that are making great inroads into the groups of credulous believers. Many such groups spent. And many still spend, one or more evenings a week getting together to study the cosmology of these "Space Brothers". Some have even channeled space brothers and written massive books that have sold well.

But let it or their, wants or needs be in conflict with ours and they are not so benevolent. The friendly "Space Brothers" suddenly are not so friendly. We, by that I mean the human race, are somehow necessary to their survival, but in a general way. Individuals, per se, are not important to them since there are so many humans to choose from. There is also evidence that this entity may have had more than a little to do with our beginnings as a race.

What is upsetting to learn, is that even though this Presence shows no true friendliness toward us, there are actually segments of the human race that have, throughout time, tried to assist this Presence in carrying out its' (or their) mission. From studying ancient records, it would seem that factions of our society have always known of the existence of this Presence, and apparently have been interacting with some of these alleged alien species, who appear to aid the Presence, for quite a while.

The inescapable conclusion is that for centuries beyond measure, humanity has been tricked and betrayed by systems and people set up and led or guided by a Presence with its' own self-interest at heart. Of course, this Presence has not had a free ride; it appears to have an opponent, equally as determined. For this reason, it seems to work through proxies, hence, the existence of secret societies.

In order to achieve what was necessary for its' own good, this Presence has used layer upon layer of conspiracies and disinformation to trick and mislead the human race. Using the promise of power, riches and glory, the Presence and its' helpers have converted numerous humans over to its' side. It is from these numerous co-opted individuals that the Presence staffs its armies and its secret societies.

There is also much evidence that the Presence has been at the bottom of the East-West problem. One item of proof, at least circumstantially, is that much of the results of the Russian research into the use of electro-magnetic weapons seems to parallel the types of electromagnetically based equipment reportedly used by the Aliens said to come from the UFOs in many of their contacts with humans. Of course, it could be that the Russian researchers just "happened" to stumble across some discoveries in this particular field and it is a coincidence, but it is amazing that their "discoveries" seem to allow them to do the same "miracles" as the flying saucers have been able to do for centuries, such as impossible cures and disabling mechanical devices[12].

This area of research will be discussed in a later chapter, but suffice it to say that for any scientific discovery, it should be possible to trace the development of the discovery through a series of earlier related projects. In other words, discoveries do not just spring forth from the alleged discoverer's head, full blown. There should be definable primitive discoveries that lead to ever more complicated discoveries. However in regard to the electro-magnetic discoveries of the Russians, in many cases, this is exactly what appears to have happened. In fact, this has happened not only in Russia, but in other countries as well.

---

12 Ostrander, Sheila and Lynn Schroeder, <u>Psychic Discoveries Behind the Iron Curtain</u>, Prentice Hall Press, New York. 1970.

You are not being asked to blindly believe what I am about to say, but I do ask that you consider my proposal just as you would a proposal from your investment advisor or your attorney. I am not asking you to invest money in anything, (other than the purchase of this book), but I am asking you to consider what I say. For if I am right, and we act to oppose the Presence, or at least smoke it out, we may have a chance of seeing the next century as a free people. If I am wrong, then we can have a good laugh and no one is hurt. Think of it as flood insurance, you may never need it, but it is better to have it and not need it than to need it and not have it.

ENTERING THE WORLD OF THE STRANGE
I am about to take you into a world that you may not be familiar with. It is a world of ancient legends, and today's headlines, of abductions and mutilations, both human and animal. Secret societies and tales of living gods. We will examine abduction reports that have not made the headlines. We will also hear from people who are afraid to come forward under their own names for fear of bodily harm. It is a journey for the strong of heart and mind. Remember, when you read of the experiences of these unfortunate, or fortunate, depending on your point of view, there but for the grace of God, go you.

It may come as a great shock to many, but the UFO research field is complex, confusing and dangerous. It also contains much in the way of valuable truth. Some of the danger comes from the Presence and its' minions. Some of the danger comes from, heretofore unknown, secret societies who serve, perhaps unknowingly, the Presence. Then too, unfortunately, some of the danger comes from our own Government. There have been numerous deaths, accidental and otherwise, among the hard core researchers. Not surprisingly, especially if my theory is correct, those who have died have been those who have seemed to be getting close to something worthwhile in their investigations.

As an aside, in addition to the over twenty witnesses to the actual assassination who died within the first few years after the event, over fifty investigators who have been involved in research that would tend to tie the assassination of John Kennedy with the UFO mystery have met violent deaths[13]. I'm not sure what that means, but it does seem to be something more than coincidence.

Incidentally, as another interesting note, there was an individual making the rounds of the talk shows and speaking on the seminar circuit, who maintained that John Kennedy was killed because he found out the truth about the shadowy organization referred to as MJ-12. In early 1963 President Kennedy was alleged to have given MJ-12 one year in which to reveal the truth to the American Public about the aliens and in addition is alleged to have ordered MJ-12 to stop government involvement in the drug trade. As a result, M-12 is supposed to have marked President Kennedy for elimination[14]. This would seem to be an area of investigation perhaps worth following, especially if your life insurance is paid up.

THE GODS CAME DOWN

According to the earliest legends of this planet, found in almost every early civilization on the planet that man was raised by a god, or gods, from his primitive state to become what he (or she) is today. Now comes the question, who were these gods? According to the Sumerians man was created in the laboratory by the Annunaki[15] to be a worker drone. Either an intention modification or a lab accident gave man the ability to procreate.

Christianity talks about the Hebrew god who created the world in six days and rested on the seventh. Of course even the biblical books seem to have some confusion regarding this concept. God is said to be the one true god, but the word used to describe him in the original Hebrew works use the word Elohim. This word is used to refer to the one god and yet Elohim is a Hebrew word which expresses concepts of divinity or deity,

---

13 Grodon, Robert J. and Harrison Edward Livingstone, HIGH TREASON, The Conservatory Press. 1989. 469 pages.

14 Cooper, Milton William, OPERATION MAJORITY, Private printing. Order from Milton William Cooper, 1311 S. Highland #205, Fullerton, CA. 92632.

[15] According to later Babylonian myth, the Annunaki were the children of Anu and Ki, brother and sister gods, themselves the children of Anshar and Kishar (Skypivot and Earthpivot, the Celestial poles), who in turn were the children of Lahamu and Lahmu ("the muddy ones"), names given to the gatekeepers of the Abzu temple at Eridu, the site at which the creation was thought to have occurred. Finally, Lahamu and Lahmu were the children of Tiamat and Abzu.

notably used as a name of God in Judaism. It is apparently related to the Northwest Semitic word Ēl which means "god". Within the Hebrew language however, Elohim is morphologically a plural, in use both as a true plural with the meaning "angels, gods, rulers" and as a "plural intensive" with singular meaning, referring to a god or goddess, and especially to the single God of Israel[16].

But Christianity is not the only religion that uses language that refers to the concept of one God actually being "gods". The ancient Sumerians talk about the creature that came from the sea to teach their remote ancestors the arts of civilization. In the *Earth Chronicles* series, author Zacharia Sitchin outlined the writings of the ancient Sumerians. According to his translations, the Sumerians believe that they were taught the rudiments of civilization by a being called Oannes.

Oannes was actually the name given by the Babylonian writer

Figure 9: Oannes

Berossus in the 3rd century BC to a supposedly mythical being who is said to have taught early mankind wisdom. Berossus describes Oannes as having the body of a fish but underneath it was said that he had the figure of a man. This being is described as dwelling beneath the waters of the

---

[16]Wikipedia

Persian Gulf. According to the Sumerian writings Oannes rose out of the waters in the daytime and furnished mankind instruction on writing, the arts and the various sciences.

The name "Oannes" was once conjectured to be derived from that of the ancient Babylonian god Ea, but it is now known that the name is the Greek form of the Babylonian Uanna (or Uan) a name used for Adapa[17] in texts from the Library of Ashurbanipal[18]. The Assyrian texts attempt to connect the word to the Akkadian for a craftsman ummanu but this is a merely a pun. Scholars have long speculated that the name might ultimately be derived from that of the 8th century figure of Jonah (Hebrew Yonah). Bible critics have made the reverse claim, although the Hebrew name has the known meaning of "dove". Oannes has historically been portrayed as a man wearing the skin of a fish. Or is it perhaps a man, or perhaps Alien, wearing a diving suit? It is a mystery, but some knew the truth.

In fact, each early civilization on this planet talked about a mysterious being that came from nowhere to teach the locals the rudiments of civilization. In each case, once the civilization began to grow in sophistication, the teacher mysteriously vanished into the mists, never

---

[17] Adapa was a mortal from a godly lineage, a son of Ea (Enki in Sumerian, a name specifically applied to one of the leaders of the Annunaki), the god of wisdom and of the ancient city of Eridu, who brought the arts of civilization to that city (from Dilmun, according to some versions). He broke the wings of Ninlil the South Wind, who had overturned his fishing boat, and was called to account before Anu. Ea, his patron god, warned him to apologize humbly for his actions, but not to partake of food or drink while he was in heaven, as it would be the food of death. Anu, impressed by Adapa's sincerity, offered instead the food of immortality, but Adapa heeded Ea's advice, refused, and thus missed the chance for immortality that would have been his.

Adapa is often identified as advisor to the mythical first (antediluvian) king of Eridu, Alulim. In addition to his advisory duties, he served as a priest and exorcist, and upon his death took his place among the Seven Sages or Apkallū. (Apkal, "sage", comes from Sumerian Abgallu (Ab=water, Gal=Great, Lu=man) a reference to Adapa, the first sage's association with water.)

[18] Ashurbanipal (Akkadian: Aššur-bāni-apli, "Ashur is creator of an heir"; 685 B.C. – c. 627 B.C.), also spelled Assurbanipal or Ashshurbanipal, was the son of Esarhaddon and the last great king of the Neo-Assyrian Empire (668 B.C. – c. 627 B.C.). He established the first systematically organized library in the ancient Middle East, the Library of Ashurbanipal, which survives in part today at Nineveh. In the Bible he is called Asenappar (Ezra 4:10).[4] Roman historian Justinus identified him as Sardanapalus

to be seen again. Suffice it to say without these mysterious teachers civilization on this planet might be very different.

But now comes some big questions, who were these teachers, where did they come from and where did they go? Of course there is the biggest question of all, were these mysterious teachers who raised the human race from the primitive jungle runners to be civilized actually the gods of antiquity?

In earlier eons, depending on your belief, God, or the gods, dealt directly with man, or at least certain representatives of man. During this same era, God, or one or more of the gods, had relations with human females and gave birth to entities part god and part mortal. These were the famous demi-gods who became the rulers of lesser mortals. These were the sons of the gods. The gods themselves seem to have pulled away from man, to oversee things from afar. So what happened? Why did the gods leave?

CHAPTER THREE
MEN IN BLACK

As outlined previously, it is the belief of this author that there exists a well-organized group of individuals, or, if you prefer, entities, that openly ruled this world at the beginning of time and now continues to control activities on the planet from behind the scenes. However, to obscure the true picture there is a great deal of misdirection that must be gotten through first.

THE ANNUNAKI

There are many legends that hold that the original visitors to this planet, those our ancestors would eventually call gods were a race referred to at the dawn of history as the Annunaki. However, historically the Annunaki (also variously referred to as: Anunna, Anunnaku, Ananaki and a number of other variations) are best known as a group of Sumerian, Akkadian and Babylonian deities. The name is variously written "da-nuna", "da-nuna-ke4-ne", or "da-nun-na", meaning something to the effect of 'those of royal blood' or 'princely offspring'.

There was another race that our ancestors look at as gods that were referred to as the Igigi. The Annunaki relation to the Igigi[19] is unclear - at

---

[19] Igigi is a term that is used to refer to the gods of heaven in Sumerian mythology

times the names are used synonymously but in the Atra-hasis flood myth the Igigi were actually part of the Annunaki only they were assigned to duty in space to overlook the planet. However, the legends also say that they rebelled after 40 days and were replaced by the creation of the human race.

Jeremy Black and Anthony Green[20] offer a slightly different perspective on the Igigi and the Annunaki, writing that "lgigu or Igigi is a term introduced in the Old Babylonian Period as a name for the (ten) 'great gods'.

While it sometimes kept that sense in later periods, from Middle Babylonian times on it is generally used to refer to the gods of heaven collectively, just as the term Anunnakku (Anuna) was later used to refer to the gods of the underworld. In the Epic of Creation, it is said that there are 300 lgigu of heaven[21]." These 300 hundred were said to be those who looked down from above or the Watchers.

These early gods, called the Anunnaki, appear in the Babylonian creation myth, *Enuma Elish*. In the later version of this myth, magnifying the great god Marduk, after the creation of mankind, Marduk divides the Anunnaki and assigns them to their proper stations, three hundred in heaven, three hundred on the earth. In gratitude, the Anunnaki, the

Figure 10: Winged Bull

"Great Gods", built Esagila, the splendid: "*They raised high the head of Esagila equaling Apsu. Having built a stage-tower as high as Apsu, they set up in it an abode for Marduk, Enlil, and Ea.*" Then they built their own shrines.

According to later Babylonian myths, the Anunnaki were the children of Anu and Ki, brother and sister gods, themselves the children of Anshar and Kishar (Skypivot and Earthpivot, the Celestial poles), who in turn were the children of Lahamu and Lahmu ("the muddy ones"), names

---

[20]Black, Jeremy and Anthony Green, Gods, demons and symbols of ancient Mesopotamia: an illustrated dictionary. London: British Museum Press, 1992.
[21]These gods of heaven are also related to the "Watchers."

given to the gatekeepers of the Abzu temple at Eridu, the site at which the creation was thought to have occurred. Finally, Lahamu and Lahmu were the children of Tiamat and Abzu two of the earliest and most senior gods.

THE MYSTERIOUS ROBED ONES

In addition to the Annunaki, there were also the mysterious teachers who spread the gift of knowledge to many of the primitive cultures on this planet. There have also been numerous other stories about individuals wearing blacked hooded robes that have appeared at various times in our history to sort of nudge history in the direction that they wanted it to go.

Figure 11: Robed figure

As one example there was Helvetius, the grandfather of the celebrated philosopher of the same name. He was an alchemist who labored ceaselessly to fathom the mystery of the "philosopher's stone," the legendary catalyst that would allow him to transmute base metals into gold.

According to a story handed down through history, one day in 1666 when he was working in his laboratory at the Hague, a stranger attired all in black, as befitted a respectable burgher of North Holland, appeared and informed him that he would remove all the alchemist's doubts about the existence of the philosopher's stone, for he himself possessed such an object.

The stranger immediately drew from his pocket a small ivory box, containing three pieces of metal the color of brimstone. With those three bits of metal, he said, he could make as much as twenty tons of gold.

The alchemist examined the pieces of metal and seeing that they were very brittle, he surreptitiously scraped off a small portion with his thumbnail. He then returned the three pieces of metal to his mysterious visitor and invited him to perform the process of transmutation. The stranger answered that he was not allowed to do so. It was enough that he had verified the existence of the metal to Helvetius. It was his purpose only to offer him encouragement in his experiments.

After the man's departure, Helvetius procured a crucible and a portion of lead, into which, when in a state of fusion, he threw the stolen grain he had secretly scraped from the alleged philosopher's stone. He was disappointed to find that the grain evaporated, leaving the lead in its original state. Thinking that he had been made a fool by the mad burgher's whimsy, Helvetius returned to his own experiments in attaining the philosopher's stone.

Some weeks later, when he had almost forgotten the incident, Helvetius received another visit from the stranger. Impatiently, the alchemist told the man that if he could not do as he claimed, then please leave the laboratory at once.

"Very well," the stranger said, consenting to perform a demonstration of the philosopher's stone for the skeptical Helvetius. "I shall show you that that which you most desire does truly exist."

The mysterious visitor said that one grain was sufficient, but it was necessary to envelope it in a ball of wax before throwing it on the molten metal; otherwise, its extreme volatility would cause it to vaporize.

To Helvetius's astonishment, the stranger transmuted several ounces of lead into gold. Then he permitted the alchemist to repeat the experiment by himself, and Helvetius converted six ounces of lead into very pure gold.

Helvetius found it impossible to keep a secret of such immense value and importance. Soon the word of the alchemist's remarkably successful experiments spread all over The Hague, and Helvetius demonstrated the power of the philosopher's stone in the presence of the Prince of Orange, and many times afterward, until he had exhausted the supply of catalytic pieces that he received from the mysterious burgher.

And search as he might, Helvetius could not find the man in all of North Holland nor learn his name. And pray as he might, the stranger never again visited Helvetius in his study. All that Helvetius was left with was the knowledge that the philosopher's stone was real.

Down through the centuries, very mysterious individuals have appeared at certain moments in human history and provided convincing demonstrations that "impossible" inventions are possible.

The "respectable burgher of North Holland" had appeared "modest and simple" to the alchemist Helvetius. It was his incredible scientific knowledge that startled and inspired the alchemists of Helvetius's day, and though these learned and determined men never did acquire the philosopher's stone that would transmute lead into gold, they did fashion the seeds of the science of chemistry that has accomplished so many transmutations of the human environment and the human condition in the last three hundred years.

While most people look at alchemy as bunk, in fact it was the study of alchemy that gave rise to many of the great scientific advances in history. It was out of the smoky laboratories of the alchemists that:

- Albert le Grand produced potassium lye
- Raymond Lully prepared bicarbonate of potassium
- Paracelsus described zinc and introduced chemical compounds in medicine
- Blaise Vigenere discovered benzoic acid
- Basil Valentine perfected sulfuric acid
- Johann Friedrich Boetticher became the first European to produce porcelain

While each of the above is an important discovery, there are rumors that lying amidst the musty pages of certain ancient alchemical laboratories there are recorded experiments with photography, radio transmission, phonography, aerial flight and numerous other areas of research.

Throughout the Middle Ages and the Renaissance, there were many scholars who claimed that they had received late-night visits from mysterious members of an unnamed secret society that had accomplished the transmutation of metals, the means of prolonging life, the knowledge to see and to hear what was occurring in distant places, and the ability to travel across the heavens in heavier-than-air vehicles.

Some students of the history of alchemy have stated that crumbling, yellowed records of the alchemists remain in dusty libraries all over the world - more than 100,000 ancient volumes written in a code that have never been sufficiently deciphered.

Numerous occult groups have been created around the belief that centuries ago a secret society achieved a very high level of scientific knowledge that they carefully guarded from the rest of humanity. According to these occultists, certain men of genius in ancient Egypt and Persia were given access to the records of the advanced technologies of the antediluvian world of Atlantis. Many hundreds of years ago, these ancient masters learned to duplicate many of the feats of the Titans of the lost continent.

There are persistent legends in nearly every culture that tell of an Elder Race that populated the Earth millions of years ago. The Old Ones, who may originally have been of extraterrestrial origin, were an immensely intelligent and scientifically advanced species who eventually chose to structure their own environment under the surface of the planet's soil and seas.

According to legend, the Old Ones usually remain aloof from the surface dwellers, but from time to time throughout history, usually at pivotal point in time, they have been known to visit certain of Earth's more intelligent members in the guise of alchemists or mysterious scientists in order to offer constructive criticism and, in some cases, to give valuable advice in the material sciences.

The Buddhists have incorporated Agharta, an ancient subterranean empire, into their theology and fervently believe in its existence and in the reality of underworld supermen who periodically surface to oversee the progress of the human race. According to one source, the underground kingdom of Agharta was created when the ancestors of the present day cave dwellers drove the Serpent People from the caverns during an ancient war between the reptilian humanoids and the ancient human society.

The decision to form an ancient secret society may have been based on the members' highly developed moral sense and their recognition of the awesome position of responsibility that the discovery of such applications of ancient knowledge had placed upon them. They may have decided to keep their own counsel until the rest of the world had become enlightened enough to deal wisely with such a high degree of technical accomplishments.

From time to time, the secret society may decide the time is propitious to make one of its discoveries known to the "outside world." Such intervention in the affairs of humankind is usually accomplished by carefully feeding certain fragments of research to "outside" scientists whose work and attitude have been judged particularly deserving. When these scientists accomplish the breakthroughs in their research, they credit the success of the experiments to their own diligence, and the secrecy the society prizes so highly is maintained.

On the other hand, the secret society may feel little or no responsibility of any kind to those humans outside of their group. They may be merely biding their time until they turn the great mass of humanity into their slaves.

By the 1840s, the legend of Agharta had already been widely circulated among the mystically minded in Germany. According to this ancient tradition, the Master of the World already controlled many of the kings and rulers of the surface world by exercising his occult powers. Soon this Master and his super race would launch an invasion of Earth and subjugate all humans to his will.

If certain master magicians, disciples of the Titans, individuals of exceptional intellect, power, and wealth, actually did achieve a high degree of technical accomplishment several centuries ago, then they could very well be responsible for a good many of the strange and mysterious vehicles seen in our skies. And if alien life-forms apprehended their advanced technology at the end of the previous century, then they might have established an alliance with the society of humans that easily appeared to be the more advanced and worthy to receive the benefits of their extraterrestrial super-science.

THE MYSTERIOUS AIRSHIP

The year 1897 may have seemed an ideal time to show the "outsiders" just how far advanced the members of the ancient secret society really were. The science of the outsiders seemed as though it had gone about as far as it could go, and it was poised confidently on the brink of the twentieth century.

Interestingly enough many of these new advancements were publically "discovered" by some of the world's most learned men and women who were filled with pride over a host of new technological accomplishments. Of course in the mind of this author, the question is whether these "learned men" were really the originator of these advancements or whether they were guided.

As an example of some of the advances that took place at this time frame:

- In 1893, Karl Benz and Henry Ford built their first four-wheeled automobiles;
- In 1889 Thomas Edison's Kinetoscope was among the first practical systems of cinematography;
- In 1895, Louis and Auguste Lumiere presented the first commercial projection;
- In that same year, Wilhelm Roentgen discovered X rays, Marconi invented radio telegraphy, and Konstantin Tsiolkovsky formulated the principle of rocket reaction propulsion;
- In 1896, William Ramsay isolated helium, Ernest Rutherford accomplished the magnetic detection of electrical waves, and Henri Becquerel discovered radioactivity;
- The Royal Automobile Club was founded in London in 1897, and cars were going faster every year;

However, with all of these scientific marvels about which to boast, there were as yet no heavier-than-air aerial vehicles to occupy the efforts and the interests of potential aviators; and a good number of brilliant scientists of great reputation had gone on record with their arguments that it was aerodynamically impossible to build such a flying machine.

On the other hand, the future of balloon transport seemed promising, and gondolas could be attached to carry passengers. With all the other wonders of modern science, how could anyone bemoan the lack of heavier-than-air flying machines?

And yet, in March of 1897, a bizarre aircraft, often described as resembling a cone-shaped steamboat, was seen flying across the United States and later throughout the world.

The German Count Ferdinand von Zeppelin did not build his famous airship, a rigid dirigible, until 1898.

Could some mysterious unknown inventors have beaten Count von Zeppelin to the drawing board with a much more impressive vehicle, a forerunner of the modern passenger plane?

Or was a secret terrestrial society of master magicians once again displaying their superiority over the outsiders?

Figure 12: Similar to the mystery airship

The flights of the enigmatic airship continued until August of 1897 when the craft was sighted off the coast of Norway and over Vancouver, British Columbia on the same day.

After a twelve-year absence, the airship reappeared over England in 1909. Within a matter of days, it was sighted over New Zealand, Arkansas, Massachusetts, Rhode Island, West Virginia, and Tennessee. Its final appearance seems to have been over Memphis on January 20, 1910.

In 1871, occultist Edward Bulwer-Lytton wrote *The Coming Race*[22], a novel about a small group of German mystics who had discovered a race of supermen living within the Earth's interior. The super race had built a paradise based on The Vril Force, a form of energy so powerful that the older beings had outlawed its use as a potential weapon. The Vril was believed to have been derived from the Black Sun, a large ball of "Prima Materia" that provided light and radiation to the inhabitants of the inner Earth.

In 1919, Karl Haushofer founded the Brothers of the Light Society in Berlin, and soon changed its name to the Vril Society.

As Haushofer's Vril Society grew in prominence, it united three major occult societies, the Lords of the Black Stone, the Black Knights of the Thule Society, and the Black Sun and chose the swastika, the hooked cross, as its symbol of the worship of the Black Sun. As with many secret

---

[22]Bulwer-Lytton, Edward, The Coming Race, 1871

groups, there appears to have been more than one order - those who followed the Golden Sun and those who followed the Black Sun.

The Black Sun, like the Swastika, is a very ancient symbol. While the Swastika represents the eternal fountain of creation, the Black Sun is even older, suggesting the very void of creation itself. The symbol on the Nazi flag is the Thule Sonnenrad (Sun Wheel), not a reversed good luck Swastika. The Black Sun can be seen in many ancient Babylonian and Assyrian places of worship.

While these societies borrowed some concepts and rites from various Hermetic groups, they placed special emphasis on the innate mystical powers of the Aryan race. The Vril and its fellow societies maintained that the Germanic/Nordic/Teutonic people were of Aryan origin, and that Christianity had destroyed the power of the Teutonic civilization.

The secret societies formed in Germany wanted desperately to prove themselves worthy of working with the super humans that lived beneath the surface of the planet and they wished to be able to control the incredibly powerful Vril force.

This ancient force was not unknown, in fact it had been known among the alchemists and magicians as,

- Chi
- Odic force
- Orgone
- Astral Light...

No matter what this force was called, those that worked with it were well aware of its transformative powers to create supermen of ordinary mortals.

The Vril Lodge believed that those who learned control of the Vril would become master of themselves, those around them, and the world itself, if they should so choose. In other words, use of this force could give one the power to rule the world.

This ability was of great interest to some members of the Lodge such as Adolf Hitler, Heinrich Himmler, Hermann Goring, and Dr.

Theodor Morell, Hitler's personal physician as well as a number of other top Nazi leaders.

In fact the Nazi leadership became obsessed with preparing German youth to become a Master Race so the Lords of the Inner Earth would find them worthy above all others when they emerged to evaluate the people of Earth's nations. There are many who believe that the Lords of the Inner Earth are the descendants of those who first colonized the earth.

In 1921, Maria Orsic (Orsitch), a medium in the Vril Society, which had now been renamed Vril Gesellschaft, began claiming spirit messages originating from Aryan aliens on Alpha Tauri in the Aldeberan star system. Through these channeled messages Orsitch and another medium that by the name of Sigrun, learned that the aliens spoke of two classes of people on their world, the Aryan, or master race and a subservient planetary race that had evolved through mutation and climate changes

According to the channeled messages, a half billion years ago, the Aryans, also known as the Elohim[23] or Elder Race, began to colonize our solar system. On Earth, the Aryans were identified as the Sumerians until they elected to carve out an empire for themselves in the hollow of the planet.

Students of the Vril Society also insist that extraterrestrials worked with Nazi scientists to create early models of flying saucers. According to some researchers, an alien tutor race secretly began cooperating with certain German scientists from the Thule, the Vril, and the Black Sun societies in the late 1920s. Working in underground bases with the alien intelligences, the Nazis mastered antigravity space flight, established space stations, accomplished time travel, an developed their spacecraft to warp speeds.

In 1922, members of Thule and Vril claim to have built the Jenseitsflugmaschine, the Other World Flight Machine, based on the psychic messages received from the Aldeberan aliens. W. O. Schulmann of the Technical University of Munich was in charge of the project until it

---

[23] An ancient Hebrew term for gods.

was halted in 1924, and the craft was stored in Messerschmitt's Augsburg. In 1937, after Hitler came into power, he authorized the construction of the Rund flugzeug, the round, or disk-shaped vehicle, for military use and for spaceflight.

In April, 1942, Nazi Germany sent out an expedition composed of a number of its most visionary scientists to seek a military vantage point in the hollow earth. Although the expedition of leading scientists left at a time when the Third Reich was putting maximum effort in their drive against the Allies, Goering, Himmler, and Hitler are said to have enthusiastically endorsed the project. Steeped in the more esoteric teachings of metaphysics, the Fuehrer had long been convinced that Earth was concave and that a master race lived on the inside of the planet.

The Nazi scientists who left for the island of Rugen had complete confidence in the validity of their quest to find an entrance to the inner world. In their minds, such a coup as discovering the opening to the Inner World would not only provide them with a military advantage, but it would go a long way in convincing the Masters who lived there that the German people truly deserved to mix their blood with them in the creation of a hybrid master race to occupy the surface world, truly a New World Order.

In 1991 when President George H.W. Bush began speaking about a New World Order to beef up his campaign for reelection, evangelist Pat Robertson, who was briefly a presidential candidate, passionately spoke out that "new world order" was actually a code for a secret group that sought to replace Christian society with a worldwide atheistic socialist dictatorship. In his view, and that of many others, there was a group working behind the scenes to bring about this dictatorship.

Bush, the conspiracy buffs charged, was a member of one of the world's most devilish and powerful secret societies: the Order of Skull and Bones. What was more, according to these same conspiracists, Bush was also linked to the Bilderbergers, the Council on Foreign Relations (CFR) and the Trilateral Commission, dangerous elitist organizations. It was also pointed out that the CFR was organized by the British Round Table Group which in turn was funded by a bequest from the Last Will and Testament of Cecil Rhodes. The purpose of this bequest was to keep the British Empire the most power country in the world.

At about the same time that President Bush's alleged secret affiliations were being exposed, a number of fundamentalist evangelists began to take their first real notice of the UFO phenomenon and saw the mysterious aerial objects as the "signs in the skies" referred to in apocalyptic literature and in the book of Revelation.

It was a short leap for many evangelists to begin to blend accounts of UFOs with the secret societies of top U.S. government officials, politicians, corporate chairmen, international bankers, and many others who sought to bring into being the dreaded "New World Order."

According to the proponents of this cosmic conspiracy, when President Ronald Reagan gave his famous "alien invasion" speech to the entire United Nations General Assembly in September of 1987, he had already secretly advised representatives of the 176 member nations that the leaders of their respective governments must meet the demands of the technologically superior extraterrestrials or be destroyed.

As Reagan said in his speech:

"I occasionally think how quickly our differences worldwide would vanish if we were facing an alien threat from outside this world. And yet I ask you, is not an alien threat already among us?"

Some UFO researchers have warned that highly placed members of an ancient secret society that can trace its origins beyond the temples of ancient Egypt to Atlantis have established a plan to create a carefully staged "alien invasion" that will convince the masses of the world that a real-life War of the Worlds alien attack is about to begin. People of all nations will believe their leaders who say that it has been learned that the aliens are a benevolent species and that unconditional surrender to them is for everyone's own good.

Immediately following the "surrender" to the aliens, the leaders of the ancient secret society will form a One World Government, a New

World Order, thus fulfilling biblical prophecies about a return to the days of Babylon.

Concern over interference by secret societies in the affairs of government was considered very real long before our present-day paranoia. For hundreds of years, certain scholars have worried about global conspiracies being conducted in secret by such groups as the Knights Templar, the Vril, the Thule, the Black Sun, and the Illuminati - who may all be waiting until the propitious time to complete world domination.

In 1876, Benjamin Disraeli, British prime minister, warned:

"The governments of the present day have to deal not merely with other governments, with emperors, kings, and ministers, but also with the secret societies which have everywhere their unscrupulous agents, and can at the last moment upset all the governments' plans."

Even those at the highest of the levels of power are well aware that there are forces operating behind the scenes that exercise tremendous power.

CHAPTER FOUR
NON-HUMANS AMONG US

If as is proposed, there are descendants of an alien race that lives among us and actually manipulates both people as well as governments, then there must over the eons been some signs of them.

John A. Keel, in his book 'Our Haunted Planet,[24]', gives an interesting introduction to the reality of an alien race that allegedly has taken careful measures to remain hidden from the mass consciousness of those dwelling on the surface of planet earth -- or those ignorant 'human cattle' whom they are intent on manipulating and exploiting from their secret hiding places above, below and even amongst the inhabitants of planet earth:

"...The parahuman Serpent People of the past are still among us. They were probably worshipped by the builders of Stonehenge and the forgotten ridge-making cultures of South America. "...

In some parts of the world the Serpent People successfully posed as gods and imitated the techniques of the super-intelligence. This led to the formation of pagan religions centered on placating these gods, and

---

[24]Keel, John, Our Haunted Planet, Galde Press, Inc.; Revised edition (May 1, 1999)

very often resulted this placation took the form of human sacrifices. The conflict, so far as man himself was concerned, became one of religions and races. Whole civilizations based upon the worship of these false gods rose and fell in Asia, Africa, and South America. The battleground had been chosen, and the mode of conflict had been decided upon.

The human race would supply the pawns to be used, and abused, in these wars of the gods. The mode of control exercised by the gods was complicated as usual. Human beings were largely free of direct control due to free will. Therefore, each individual had to consciously commit himself, or herself, to one of the opposing forces. As a result, the main battle became one for control of what we call the human soul.

Sumerian goddess figurine from Ubaid (Mesopotamia, c. 5000 BC).

Figure 13: Serpent People

Once an individual had committed himself, or herself, to a particular belief, he opened a door of some sort so that an indefinable something could actually enter his body and exercise some control over his subconscious mind.

Many researchers believe that what became known as the Serpent People or OMEGA Group, attacked man in various ways, trying to rid the planet of him. But the super-intelligence was still able to look over man. God worked out new ways of communication and control, always in conflict with the Serpent People. There are a number of researchers who have claimed that the story of the serpent in the Garden of Eden actually referred to one of the Serpent People.

There have also been a number of stories told in relation to these 'Serpent People', maintaining that some of these creatures are now living among us and have been doing so for a very long time. There is an individual who is believed to be an anonymous Intelligence officer who is referred to as 'Commander X'. He has recently released details of an incident which may well have come right out of a John Carpenter movie, if not for the fact that the Commander himself, from his own high-security position within the Intelligence Community, is convinced of its potential reality:

Another story comes from a service member, a private, stationed on the surface at Dulce, New Mexico. Though most privates tend to mind their own business, this young man soon realized something mighty 'odd' was going on around there, but it took a while for him to put his finger on it. According to a statement that the private later gave to several researchers who put him in touch with Commander X:

"*'One morning last September, I was working on a routine job when another of the young enlistees, a mechanic, came in with a small rush job he wanted welded at once. He had the print and proceeded to show me exactly what he wanted. We are both bending over the bench in front of the welder when I happened to look directly into his face. It seemed to suddenly become covered with a semi-transparent film or cloud. His features faded and in their place appeared a 'thing' with bulging eyes, no hair and scales for skin. I stood and looked at it for about 20 seconds. Whatever it was stood and looked at me without moving. Then the strange face seemed to fade away, and at the same time recede into the ordinary face of the young man underneath. The dissipation of the imposed face lasted or took about five seconds before it was completely gone and I was standing there weak, my mouth open and staring at the young man who had come in with the rush order. The young 'man' did not seem to be conscious of the elapsed time when I had observed all this but went right on talking about the job as if nothing had happened.*"

"*'This is hard to take but I assure you it was still harder for me. No one can realize a jolt you could get from seeing anything like this until they have experienced it for themselves. It was several days before I had myself convinced that maybe after all what I had seen was real and that I was not suffering from illusions and the beginning of insanity. Days passed before I saw this particular phenomenon again. The next time was later at night at the guard house near the front gate, on the way to work. I had purchased some small items and on arriving I went around to the guard house with my slip to retrieve my package. There was only one guard on duty. I handed him the check and he began to look at the package, taking his time. I waited a minute, and then happened to look directly at him again. His face began to change. Again a face of a strange creature was imposed. You could see through the imposed face for a few seconds and then it became the only one visible [solidified is the word] and again about 20 seconds duration. Again five seconds for dissipation and the guard started to move normally again, found my package and gravely handed it to me and I walked out without a word being said.'"*

Since coming across this report from the 'Commander', a number of researchers have made an effort to see if there were any other similar accounts that might confirm the existence of 'Chameleons' or alien 'infiltrators' working on the surface of planet earth in an apparent attempt to pass themselves off as human beings and blend-in with our society, for whatever nefarious agenda they might be serving. Some of the reports of quasi-human infiltrators spoke of the "Men In Black" who have terrorized UFO witnesses. Although many of the 'M.I.B.' who have been reported were obviously humans working for some obscure governmental surface, other-planetary or subterranean intelligence agency as well as others that appeared to be either cyborgs, clones or even paraphysical manifestations, there was a branch of the so-called MIB which betrayed definite reptilian characteristics.

These in essence were reptilian humanoids with a full-blown -- although at times not-too-convincing -- 'reconstructive surgery' job, apparently intended to allow them to operate in human society undetected. Some of the early 'infiltrators' betrayed themselves with their 'plastic' or artificial appearance, whereas in more recent years the 'disguise' has become far more sophisticated with the advent of molecular shape-shifting occult-technology, techno-hypnotic transmitters, and portable laser-hologram technology, and as a result, they are harder to detect. However there are ways.

George Andrews, in his book *Extraterrestrial Friends and Foes*,[25] quotes a statement made by Valdamar Valerian, director of Leading Edge Research:

"A friend of mine and four of his friends experimented with crystalline structures a year or two ago (mid-1980's - Branton), and they figured out how to cut them along certain planes so they could actually see the aura or energy field around people. That's when they discovered that all people aren't 'people', or the people they thought they were. It appears that some E.T. humanoids have a dark blue ovoid aura. (Note: Aura cameras developed by Chuck Shramek -- the same Chuck Shramek of the 'Hale-Bopp Companion' controversy -- and others clearly show the 7 multi-colored 'chakra' points of the human soul/spirit matrix. Presumably since reptilians have NO soul, they would have NO multicolored auric field.) It so happens that all the people they checked that met these criteria also wore dark glasses and made every attempt to act like they really wanted nothing to do with people in general.

"They followed one of these people out into the desert where he evidently had a trailer. After waiting until dusk, they made a pretense of needing help and knocked on the door. After a short while, the light went on and the man came to the door. He looked normal, except that his pupils were vertical slits instead of circles. It works. The only trouble is that it costs $2,000 to put a pair of those glasses together..."

There have been a lot of stories that several areas across the Western U.S. where surface and/or underground military installations exist have reportedly produced similar 'Chameleon' sightings. There seems to be a trend which involves the infiltration of the NSA-CIA and the subsequent 'replacement' of agency personnel, and in turn military-Industrial personnel, by alien life forms not loyal to planet earth nor to the

---

[25] Andrews, George, Extraterrestrial Friends and Foes, ILLUMINET PRESS., P.O. Box 2808., Lilburn, GA 30226.

human race in general. These reports are very similar to other reports that made the rounds within 'fringe' research groups during the early 1980's concerning the reported 'assimilation' of high-ranking Communist officials and scientists by serpent-like humanoids, reptilian beings that were reputedly revived out of suspended animation from a frozen city that was discovered under the northern Siberian ice fields. This incident was referred to as the "Siberian Affair".

Aside from Dulce, New Mexico and the Nevada Test Site, other areas where these "chameleon" sightings are said to have taken place include Deep Springs, CA and Dugway, Utah. Dugway Proving Ground (DPG) is a US Army facility located approximately 85 miles southwest of Salt Lake City, Utah in southern Tooele County and just north of Juab County. A woman by the name of Barbara, who worked as a hair stylist at a salon near the proving grounds claimed she saw one of the high ranking military officials transform temporarily into an entity with 'reptilian' features.

Another source at Dugway who worked in an auto shop claimed that he saw a similar phenomenon while changing the tires on the car of one Dugway military official. Remember that Dugway works closely with Area 51, which is just to the west and across the state border in Nevada. It is interesting that there are claims that the joint CIA-alien activity within the 'Dreamland' underground complexes of Nevada have and are being extended to the underground facilities below the St. George and Dugway areas of Utah, among other sites.

Another 'sighting' of these shape shifters is said to have occurred just south of the mid-point of an old toll road that ran between Hopland and Lakeport, California. The sighting involved large black automobiles[26] that would leave and enter a dead-end road in the area. When investigated, the tire tracks ran right up and under a large boulder at the base of a cliff and seemingly disappeared beneath it. Since the road was fenced on one side and a steep hill existed on the other, it is unlikely that the large automobiles were able to turn around.

---

[26] Many reported Men In Black sightings are said to involve 1949 black Cadallics.

This same area, especially one particular mountain there, is known as a very unusual place. 'Bottomless' caves with stone stairwells have been reported by explorers. Government vehicles and personnel have 'disappeared' without a trace on the road. An 'atmosphere of fear' is said to exist in an area approximately 30 miles in diameter. Also there have been a lot of unexplained deaths among the settlers in the area. Apparently this area is the site of a large underground center of 'alien' activity. This activity was taking place back in the 1930's, long before the so-called alien "Men In Black" started getting any major attention from Ufologists in America.

Figure 14: Mothman

The Dulce enigma [and the "chameleons"] have not only infiltrated Utah, Nevada and California, but seems to have stretched its tentacles all the way up to the Pacific Northwest. One area of particular interest is the Madigan Military Hospital south of Seattle, Washington near FORT LEWIS... which has been investigated by Val Valerian. In June of 1992 Valerian released the following article, titled "*ALIEN INFILTRATION OF THE MILITARY MEDICAL SYSTEM: MADIGAN HOSPITAL IN WASHINGTON*", in his LEADING EDGE newsletter. According to the report:

"About a year ago, we ran into several people who stated that they 'had heard' that 'reptilian humanoids were working at a U.S. Army Hospital near Fort Lewis, Washington. At that point, these statements were simply filed away in 'rumor' status, pending the arrival of something more substantial. Descriptions of the nature of and appearance of alien humanoid forms that could be termed 'reptilian' vary widely. Reptilian humanoids have been described in Italy as looking very lizard like, even some with tails. Pictures showing some of these entities were published in an Italian magazine and eventually ended up in the United States in 'The Leading Edge'.

"Logic would seem to tell us that if alien humanoids were in fact in 'collusion' with military medical personnel at a hospital, they would not in

fact have the appearance of anything other than humans, or be close enough to humans to blend in. About a month ago, the nature of synchronicity brought me to an espresso bar, where I chanced to engage a lady in her early 50's in some small conversation about an entirely unrelated matter. She had been a nurse for some twenty years, and sixteen of those twenty years had been spent working for the U.S. Army. She retired from the service and was now job hunting in the local area. She was very professional, and seemed to know a lot about the nursing field.

Gradually, her (for ease of understanding let's call her Betty) conversation got around to a 'very unusual place', Madigan Military Hospital, which is located on Route 5 south of Seattle. She had applied for work at the hospital and noticed that it was indeed a hospital unlike any she had ever seen before. Madigan is a brand new $150 million dollar facility, built about a year or so ago. From her description, there are small R2D2-type robots that shuttle prescriptions between floors; all the equipment is prototype 'one-of-a-kind', like laser x-rays and a lot of equipment that was extremely high tech. It was not this alone which peaked my interest, but a comment she made later. She made the statement that when she entered a specific lab in the hospital, she noticed that all the personnel were extremely absorbed in their work -- nothing too uncommon about that. But then she stated that she had the thought that some of the equipment looked quite 'alien', and two men who looked exactly alike turned and looked at her in response to her thought. She said that the eyes of these two men were quite penetrating and that they both seemed to move in unison. That got Val's interest. She then stated that during the tour of the facility, the individual who was escorting her said

Bldg 9040
Fitzsimmons Drive
Tacoma, WA 98431

Directory Assistance
(253) 968-1110 DSN 782

Figure 15: Madigan Military Medical Center

that the top floor of the hospital and two of the sub-basement floors were Top Secret Research and Development areas and were off limits to both military and civilian personnel. That really got Val's attention.

"Subsequently," continued the article, "Val ran into a cable repairman who was installing cable TV in a nearby town, and decided on a hunch to mention to him about the strange nature of Madigan. The hunch paid off. He said he had been involved in the installation of fiber optic networks between the floors of the hospital when it was in its construction stage, and that there was a three foot space in between the floors where the optics ran.

"Since these observations were the result of her [the nurse Betty's] preliminary interview, Val talked to her about the idea of getting more information, since she would be going back at least one more time. She agreed to make some tapes of her observations. The transcript of these tapes is as follows:

VISIT TO MADIGAN HOSPITAL

The entrance to Madigan hospital is off of Interstate 5 past Olympia, Washington. The exit is marked as 'Madigan Hospital, Camp Murray Exit'. As you enter the area the hospital sits to the right -- a massive white structure. As you enter the parking lot, there is a pond and sunken area that runs through a bridge which connects the 'medical mall' area to a three story building that serves as the main core of the hospital, where the services like x-ray, nuclear medicine and other services are performed.

The three story complex is connected to an eight-story tower dubbed 'the nursing tower. The tower has a floor that is closed off, and Betty was never able to find access to it. (What follows are Betty's words)"

"'I entered the front of the hospital, and the lobby was very typical, but not typical of a hospital of this size. I then went to the information desk and was greeted by an 'oriental' Specialist 4th Class, who was seated. He seemed very low key and laid back. I was directed to Human Resources.

"'As I walked through the corridors, I noticed how beautiful and calm I was beginning to feel. The colors are very soft and conducive to feeling mellow.

"'The military personnel were very slow moving [which has NOT been my experience in the past, having served five years as an Army nurse], and low key. I went to the Human Resources and asked about an application, and was directed to a Master Sergeant who was the director of personnel.

"'Having been a medical technologist for the better part of 25 years, the equipment I saw at the hospital was far beyond anything I have ever seen. I was shown an area where there was a long room with computer banks on both sides where both civilian and military personnel were working. Before entering the room, I was asked to stand in front of the door, where I was scanned by some beam-like light. I was told that my thermal pattern was being recorded in order to permit my entry to the room.

"'Off this room was another room where procedures were conducted on patients, and I noticed that a patient walked over and climbed on an exam table. The procedure they were doing always requires that the patient must be sedated, however I noticed that they physician leaned over the patient and touched the patient in the center of the forehead with his index and middle finger of one hand. Immediately, the patient fell into a state off sedation and the procedure was started. What kind of doctor can touch a patient in that way and sedate him?

"'I looked around at the other personnel in the room at this time. There were two, a Private First Class and a Specialist 4th Class at opposite ends of the room from where I was standing. Both of these men were the same size, had the same skin color and moved in a very deliberate manner. I was talking with the Sergeant and happened to say something to myself very softly while having the thought how strange these people seemed. Both of the men turned and looked at me almost as if to stare at me. I got this very strange feeling.

I had heard before from a friend whose brother had made the uncharacteristic comment that 'aliens worked at Madigan. All the people in the room and the military personnel in general that I had seen in the hospital seemed to move very, very slowly, almost in slow motion. I left the area and went back to the Sergeant's office.

"'A month later, I returned to Madigan with a friend to see, without telling her anything of my experience, if she saw and felt the same things I did. She is very sensitive to variations in electromagnetic fields, and eventually had a headache and became nauseated. There are many other things about this place. Between the floors there are spaces where small robots move to deliver supplies to all the wards and other areas in the hospital, according to the Sergeant. I was told that there is no reason for personnel to go into these areas -- that the robots do all that. I did see one of the robot devices. It looked like the R2D2 character on 'star wars'.

"'My friend and I entered through what is known as the clinic mall. This area houses the outpatient clinic. There were very few people there for such a large clinic. We were told that there are three floors beneath the hospital and one floor above that are off limits to all personnel, military and civilian, and that these areas were classified Top Secret and were research and development [R&D] areas. There are very unusual antennas on top of the hospital. The three-story main service area has a complex on top of it that appears to have no entrance and no windows. Judging from the way the hospital is built, there are a lot of 'dead areas' that comprise spaces that cannot be accessed from the main service area.
"'The personal feeling we both got being in the hospital was that we started to feel very drained, and we both experienced a dull headache. It wasn't until we had driven several miles from the facility that we started to feel better.'"

In the research for this book, this author came across yet another report suggesting that reptiloid entities were infiltrating our military-industrial complex, however the exact source of this particular story was not confirmed and therefore should be taken as is. The report stated that sometime during the 1980's a young lady working as a secretary in the Pentagon noticed a high-ranking Pentagon 'official' who had apparently lost a contact lens. A quick glimpse showed her that the eye from where the lens fell out was not human, but instead contained a vertically-slit pupil. No one working at the Pentagon seemed to know where the high ranking official that had lost the contact lens worked although everyone he came in contact with had apparently assumed that he was supposed to be there in some capacity or another.

The Secretary however informed her superiors of the strange incident, and immediately Security Personnel approached the 'officer' who apparently was not aware of his missing contact lens. The 'man' did not make any major attempts to resist. According to reports the secretary heard later, when the apartment of this 'official' was searched, copies of several sensitive documents on the "Star Wars" or "Strategic Defense Initiative" program were discovered. Apparently the entity had been stealing the documents and transmitting their contents to some point beyond the planet. Rumor had it that the entity was physically examined and it was discovered that its internal organs were not human.

In reference to the Draconian interest in our planetary defense net, let's look at the following information from British Ufologists Timothy Good[27], who described the unfortunate fate of several experts who assisted in the development of the Star Wars (SDI) defense system. Apparently, they were either eliminated by those they worked for so that they would not reveal what they knew, or someone or something 'else' that was not pleased with the ultimate products of their efforts was responsible for their tragic deaths. Certainly, all of these scientists dying at once cannot be explained in coincidental terms, whatever the case:

"Reports of suspicious deaths, darkly and deeply linked to UFO's, persist, however, and continue to cause speculation. Word comes from Gordon Creighton, editor of the informative Flying Saucer Review, who notes a possible deathly tie-in with the U.S. 'Star Wars' program. He wrote to Timothy Good in Nov. 1988 as follows:

"*'here in Britain 22 scientists have reportedly either taken their own lives or died in very strange or mysterious circumstances. And it seems that most... were engaged in British work on behalf of, or related to the U.S. 'Star Wars' program. The British government, it seems, was trying*

---

[27] Good, Timothy, Need to Know: UFOs, the Military, and Intelligence, Pegasus Books (November 15, 2007).

to hush it up. But press statements here say that the U.S. government had put our government on the spot and demanded a full inquiry. So, quite clearly, it is either the Russians or THEM...'

"As many researchers have surmised, 'Star Wars', ostensibly conceived as a defensive system against Russian missile attack, may have had from its beginning a 'defensive' UFO connection. Whatever the case, a 'mock test' in September, 1988, of an earth-shattering warhead -- much like 'Star Wars' in reverse -- was conducted at the Tonopah Test Range in Nevada. Announced as a proposed super-weapon designed to destroy 'Russian' underground command centers dug in solid rock down to 1,000 [feet], some UFO analysts believe that the real target is not Russian but another adversary deep down in cavernous installations in Nevada and New Mexico.

"According to the Pentagon, the proposed earth-penetrating warhead is 'urgently needed'. According to rumor-mills, an alien race -- the 'grays' -- in their fortified underground laboratories, are genetically experimenting with the human race. Even more ominous, rumors say that their intransigence today may lead to new perils tomorrow."

MORE MEN IN BLACK STORIES

In reference to the "Chameleons" and certain elements of the so-called "Men In Black" phenomena, the following account from Brazil puts everything in perspective. The following excerpts were taken from a report by Brazilian researcher Antonio Huneeus, titled: "THE 'CHUPAS' -- UFO HORROR STORIES FROM BRAZIL". Mr. Huneeus describes the following incident that was investigated by APEX[28] in Sao Paulo, one of the best known UFO groups in Brazil, founded by Dr. Max Berezowsky:

"...The affair began near Vitoria, the capitol of [the] state of Espiritu Santo north of Rio state, where there are beaches rich in mineral contents. It happened either in late 1979 or early 1980, [Osni] Schwarz wasn't sure, when he told the story in 1986...

"A youngster called Aeromar sold beverages at the beach, where one day he encountered three men dressed with suits and tie -- highly

---

[28] Association of Extraterrestrial Investigations

unusual clothing for the beach, especially in Brazil -- who approached him and said they wanted to talk to him. Aeromar became scared, thinking they were perhaps policemen who wanted to implicate him in a drug case, so he avoided the beach for a few days. As he returned home after dropping off his girlfriend one night, he saw a car with the same three men inside. He ran to the house, but suddenly he couldn't hear well. His mother took him to the hospital where he was not cured, although about a month later he suddenly could hear well again.

"Aeromar moved to Rio, finding work at a bakery in a shift between 4 and 11 PM. One night, as he was crossing one of the many TUNNELS that link the Rio bays, he saw two of the MIB's walking in his direction. The youngster ran in the opposite direction, only to find the third MIB waiting at a bus stop. He escaped and went back to the bakery, where he told his boss that the Vitoria police were chasing him. The boss accompanied him to the nearest police station to make a complaint, which he did, but he was not believed. The boss then convinced him that he should perhaps move to Sao Paulo, a bigger city where it may be easier to go unnoticed.

"So Aeromar moved to Sao Paulo, finding work in an electrical company and sharing a room with another man. He also became friends with a vendor of beverages from Vitoria who had a stand near a movie theater. While hanging out there one night, a car stopped right in front of the stand and the door opened.

"Even though he didn't want to go, Aeromar lost his will and entered the car. The door closed and he found inside -- not surprisingly -- the three same men whom he had been dodging for months. They drove for a while, leaving the city and entering a wooded area.

"The car stopped and they all walked up to a big UFO surrounded by some sort of luminous ring and hovering above the ground. The men walked underneath the craft, which emitted a ray of light and they suddenly were inside. Still drained of any willpower, Aeromar walked to a chair and sat down. From the arms of the chair appeared handles that secured his wrists. An iron bar then pressed his forehead backwards while another gadget fastened his neck. Up to here the men were always dressed with suits, but at this point an incredible transformation took place: the MIB'S head ripped opened into a heart shape and the skin became green and scaled like a Reptilian. Take into account that while the popular image of the MIB was well known 14 years ago, the idea of reptilian abductors was then not in vogue as nowadays.

"Be that as it may, the Ufonauts proceeded to interrogate and tell him things that were going to happen both to him and the earth. To make the story even more 'Hollywoodesque', a door in the room opened at one point and Aeromar was able to peek at human corpses hanging by their feet from hooks. The man naturally became traumatized, remembering only that his straps were loosened. Everything went blank after that...

"Aeromar's conscious recollection places him next back at the theater, but several hours later since there was no traffic in the streets. He returned to his room in panic and began to tell the story to his roommate. A strange force pushed his body, however, throwing it against the wall in front of him, as he remembered the aliens had told him that he shouldn't speak about the experience or he would suffer. Aeromar cried for a while, not knowing what to do. A few days later, his friend contacted the Globo TV network, which was working on a UFO documentary. Globo, in turn, passed the tip to Dr. Max Berezowsky. Aeromar and his roommate went to APEX on a very busy day when the office was full of people. They told the whole story to Dr. Berezowsky and a few assistants, Osni Schwarz among them.

"Berezowsky attempted to do hypnotic regression with the witness, but there was too much interference in the office and Aeromar was in total panic. He was saying that 'they' were going to take him on the next Thursday and that a UFO was going to land in a Sao Paulo neighborhood on Tuesday night. A crowd of people, in fact, went that night to the supposed landing site but nothing happened. Although Dr. Berezowsky was in touch with Aeromar, He vanished a few days later and nobody ever saw him again.'"

So after all of this is it possible that this is the secret that is at the core of the ultimate secret society and thus motivates all secret societies. This secret would seem to be that over us, and among us it seems, is a more advanced race of being who earlier were treated as gods. So what are these secret societies working for? Perhaps it is the complete and total control of the human race, a control that they had firm in hand eons ago.

CHAPTER FIVE
UNITED STATES SECRETS

The breaking away from England and the founding of our Federal Government seemed, at the time, to be a heroic act of a free people. Unfortunately, these heroic acts have led to the creation of one of the most powerful governmental mechanisms in the history of the world. The power of our government penetrates right into the marital bedroom and into the most private of activities between human adults. Branches of our government monitor our every financial move, traces every transaction that we undertake, reads our mail and even monitors our every electronic (telephone, telegraph, etc.) conversation. Almost every private group has an undercover agent from some government agency as a member. As an example, at one point in Washington D.C., it was impossible to find a Communist, outside of the Embassies or the United Nations; they would all turn out to be undercover F.B.I. Agents. Is this what we call freedom? Are these the acts of a government of the people, by the people and for the people? Or are these acts of a government that does not trust its' own citizens? A Government, perhaps, with something to hide?

I spoke earlier of secret societies controlling national governments, well; it would appear that this includes the U.S. Government as well. I would point out that almost every one of the Founding Fathers belonged to one or more secret societies, such as the Masons or The Golden Dawn to name but two[29]. This brings to mind a most interesting question. Did the Founding Fathers decide of their own free will to break away from Britain, or did they have "guidance"? It is interesting to note that almost every one of the Founding Fathers was deeply involved in one way or another, in what might be referred to as the esoteric arts.

Additionally, now comes a very important question. How did a few thousand ragtag colonists and the famed minute men defeat the most powerful country on earth? It is strange to consider that the senior leaders on both the British and the Colonist sides were members of the same secret societies. Could this interesting fact that the leaders of both sides were members of the Masonic order have had something to do with the victory of the Colonial Army?

As you shall see, there is a great deal of evidence that many of the monumental changes going on during this same time period seemed to have a slight "push" from outside influences. Keep in mind as you read, this possibility: Are we carrying out someone else's master plan for the structure of our civilization?

Most of us think of a secret society as an organization whose very name is shrouded in secrecy, unfortunately, this is not always so. Sometimes, a secret society can exist right in the midst of a populated metropolis, with its' name on the door and its' charter available for the asking. However, this does not mean that there is not an inner sanctum, with its' own separate agenda. For example, there is the current Council on Foreign Relations, an organization that is routinely mentioned in the news, and whose membership includes some of the most famous people in our country. Most who know of it think that it is a governmental think tank. Few know the truth[30].

THE COUNCIL ON FOREIGN RELATIONS

---

[29] Allen, Gary and Larry Abraham, NONE DARE CALL IS CONSPIRACY. Double A Publications, Suite 403, 18000 Highway South, Seattle, Washington 98188.

[30] Ibid.

The Council on Foreign Relations (CFR) was founded in 1919 by a group on Industrialists and Internationalists, who felt that world power was best consolidated into a few hands and that their hands were the best to hold the reins of power. The CFR is one of the largest totally American "secret societies". Its charter specifically states that it is working for a new world order. This new world order is specifically a one world government. A most interesting position for an allegedly patriotic group of Americans to take[31].

Figure 16: Council on Foreign Relations

Though this organization is a privately chartered "club", if you will, its' influence reaches into almost every function of government. President Reagan appointed many members of the CFR to important positions in his administration. President Bush, a member of the CFR himself, is continuing this policy. In other words, the members of an organization who advocate the actual merging of our government with others, or the actual overthrow of our government are running our government. Some of the best known people in this country are members of this organization. A review of these names is very enlightening reading.

The history of the CFR makes even more interesting reading. The nucleus of people who ultimately formed the current inter-related secret societies were actually funded in 1891 using money left by Cecil Rhodes, famed multi-millionaire of South African fame and the gentleman after whom Rhodesia was named. Rhodes, it seems was moved by the idea of a "new world order", the creation of which became his main goal in life. For this purpose, upon his death, his massive fortune was left to be used for the

---

31 Ibid.

purpose of forming an organization to make his dream a reality. With this money, an organization was formed in England called The Round Table[32].

THE ROUND TABLE GROUP

The Round Table was organized in order to allow the would-be world leaders to join forces and fortunes in order to be able to manipulate populations on a global scale. Members of this group worked diligently to upset the world order in existence at that time. The mere fact that their actions led directly to the deaths of millions upon millions of innocent people did not stop them from moving forward for "the good of all". In fact, it was a member of this group, Jacob Schiff, who with the assistance of the famous American Family, the Rockefellers, financed the Russian Revolution. This revolution has, of course, led to the enslavement of millions and the deaths of untold millions more.

It is also true that both Lenin and Trotsky received direct assistance from elements of the U.S. Government in arriving in Russia and in raising the funds necessary to finance the Revolution[33]. This assistance was given to the Communist Movement in spite of the fact that this movement had as its' target the head of an allied government helping fight the Germans. It also is amusing that even though at war with each other, the Germans assisted the United States in helping get Lenin and his followers across Germany and into Russia. Consider the implications.

The Round Table acts through several front organizations. In England it works the Royal Institute of International Affairs; in the U.S. it became the Council on Foreign Relations. The Council on Foreign Relations, in turn, gave birth to the Trilateral Commission[34]. At the heart of each of the organizations was the undying desire to form one world government with themselves as the leaders. A dream shared by Adolf Hitler, Napoleon and hundreds of other would be dictators. Unfortunately, the members of these organizations currently hold both the financial means

---

32 Ibid.
33 Ibid.
34 Ibid.

and the political power to achieve their dream. A very dangerous and deadly combination.

INTERNATIONAL BANKERS

The most disturbing part is that on both sides, or rather all sides of this conflict, if you dig deep enough, you find International Merchant Bankers; specifically a group that was headed by the International Banking Firm of Rothschild. It was Rothschild money that financed both sides of, not only the Russian Revolution, but several other major conflicts, as well[35]. Later, I will show how this ties into my theory.

Now of course, at this point you are asking yourself what an organization dedicated to creating a one world government has to do with UFOs, aliens and abductions. Well, if my theory is right, I would suggest that there is a great deal in common between this and other similar organizations and UFOs, aliens and abductions. You may think that I am way off base, but I would suggest that we are dealing with just the tip of a major conspiracy. One that is directed at not just forming a one world government, but with total world control, right down to directing who you will marry and where you will live.

THE OCCULT CONNECTION

The founding of our great nation was, as I mentioned, shrouded in mysterious and psychic events, most of which were never known by the average person. The late 1700's appeared to be a time of great change, not only for the fledgling United States, but for most of the rest of the world as well. These changes not only effected governments, but human consciousness as well. People who for centuries had loyally served a King or other hereditary ruler suddenly felt the need to overthrow these forms of government in favor of a self-rule system. In most cases, this meant that in the space of a few years, they were being ruled by dictatorial forms of government. Dictatorial forms of government that upset the balance of life on this planet. Most convenient if you are a group who thrives on confusion and chaos.

---

35 Ibid.

As part of my research, I examined the history of many secret societies. There was one that appeared to be tied up with numerous of the rebellions that were spreading across the globe during this time period. This was The Illuminati[36].

Founded on May 1, 1776, by Adam Weishaupt, this secret order has been both dismissed as a gathering of kooks and also feared as a diabolical force for chaos and confusion. In looking for the power beyond this secret order, authorities could never quite find the true source from whence sprang the influence of this former Jesuit student. Some said that the Jesuits created the society; others said that it was the House of Rothschild, while still others felt that it was the Cabalistic Jews[37]. Whoever did organize this secret society, they planned well and it has lasted to this day as a force to be reckoned with behind the scenes of power.

There has been so much rumor and mystical mishmash written about the founding of this secret order that it is hard to know the truth. However, there is one thing that is known, The Illuminati has a connection with The Knights Templar, a military monastic order very active in the Holy Lands that was crushed by Philip the Fair of France for alleged trafficking with the forces of Darkness[38]. This connection was shown during the initiation of Count Cagliostro into the Illuminati.

According to the Count, during the initiation, which took place near Frankfort, he was shown a book. On the first page was written an oath that began "*We the Grand Masters of the Templars*". The basic outline of the book was that the Illuminati were an organization designed to topple thrones and move for a one world government. The first target would be the Monarchy of France and then Rome, in the form of the Catholic Church. In other words, the goals of the Illuminati are the same goals as the Council on Foreign Relations, and the Round Table Groups; consolidation of all the world under one government[39].

---

36 Baigent, Michael and Richard Leigh, THE TEMPLE AND THE LODGE, Arcade Publishing, New York. 1989.

37 Ibid.

38 Ibid.

39 Allen, Gary and Larry Abraham, NONE DARE CALL IS CONSPIRACY. Double A Publications, Suite 403, 18000 Highway South, Seattle, Washington 98188.

According to his account, Count Cagliostro was also made privy to the funding of the secret order. He found, and reported, that there were massive amounts of money spread all over Europe. In fact there was so much money available, that it was obvious that there had to be backing from some of the great banking houses of the world. He was of the impression that there was involvement on the part of the House of Rothschild[40].

According to the reports from the time in question, Weishaupt planned to destroy the effects of Christianity. He hated this religion because its' individualist outlook was opposed to his pantheistic-collectivism. Weishaupt seemed to feel that the worship of the One God, with a hatred taught for a slightly less powerful Satan was an incorrect application of the ancient teachings. Under his theory, which is held by almost every secret society that I could find record of, pantheism, the belief in a unity force, and its extension, duality, the belief in a unifying force, are actually different expressions for the same force. But this concept is opposed to the basis of the Christian Religion. However, it does support my theory of the solution of the UFO mystery.

---

[40] THE CONSPIRACY TRACKER, Issue No. 1, September, 1983.

CHAPTER FIVE
MEN OF DISTINCTION

The activities of a secret order may work to change the existing social order, but the activities must be carried out by individuals who are willing to see everything they hold dear destroyed. Either these men are psychopathic and knowingly take steps to destroy the world as they know it or they unknowingly act as the cat's paw of the secret order.

THE COMMUNIST MANIFESTO AND THE FORCES OF DARKNESS?

In each upheaval that took place during the last part of the 18th century, there were reports of black robed, or black clad figures making contact with the leaders of the various rebel groups. In each case, the mysterious figures aided or supplied the rebel forces with something that would assist their cause. In other words, the activities of the black garbed figures changed the existing order, reducing the power and control of the kings and emperors.

I do not claim that the Illuminati were involved in each and every one of these wars, but historical records do name them as causing or aiding the outbreak of several world changing upheavals, such as the French Revolution. However, the Illuminati was only one of several secret societies whose history stretched back over centuries. Secret Societies that seemed to have a secret to protect and carried out programs according to some master plan. A master plan where the deaths of millions were unimportant and the destruction of the world order was the goal[41].

---

41 Baigent, Michael and Richard Leigh, THE TEMPLE AND THE LODGE, Arcade Publishing, New York. 1989.

There is another interesting footnote to this particular secret society. Adam Weishaupt wrote a document that set up an organization for taking over the world. When the Bavarian police smashed the Illuminati Organization in 1786, it was thought that his plans died with his organization. However, some seventy years later an organization calling itself the League of Just Men hired a radical writer named Karl Marx to update and formalize the plans of Adam Weishaupt. Marx published these plans under the title of the Communist Manifesto. Later research showed that the League of Just Men appeared to fade from existence after the publication of the Communist Manifesto. Many seem to believe that the League of Just Men was merely the Illuminati operating under a different name[42].

Figure 17: Karl Marx

Did Marx write his own ideas, or was he instructed in what to say. Prior to the publication of the Communist Manifesto, Marx had not expressed such ideas, though he was somewhat known to have radical ideas. Karl Heinrich Marx was born in Trier, in the Kingdom of Prussia's Province of the Lower Rhine. His father, Heinrich Marx, was born a Jew but converted to Lutheranism prior to Karl's birth to advance his career as a lawyer. A man of the Enlightenment, Heinrich was devoted to Kant and Voltaire, who took part in agitations for a constitution in Prussia. Karl's mother, born Henrietta Pressburg, was from the Netherlands, and Jewish at the time of Karl's birth, although she converted upon the death of her parents. Karl was baptized when he was six years old. Interestingly, very little is known about Marx's childhood.

Karl Marx married very well. He wife was Jenny von Westphalen, the educated daughter of a Prussian baron, on June 19, 1843 in the Pauluskirche, at Bad Kreuznach. Marx and Jenny had seven children, but

---

42 Allen, Gary and Larry Abraham, NONE DARE CALL IT CONSPIRACY, Double A Publications, Suite 403, 18000 Highway South, Seattle, Washington 98188.

due to poverty, only three survived to adulthood. Marx didn't have a lot of assets. His major source of income was from the support of Friedrich Engels, who was drawing a steadily increasing income from the family business in Manchester. This was supplemented by weekly articles written as a foreign correspondent for the New York Daily Tribune. Inheritances from one of Jenny's uncles and her mother who died in 1856 allowed the family to move to somewhat better lodgings at 9 Grafton Terrace, Kentish Town a new suburb on the then-outskirts of London. Marx generally lived a hand-to-mouth existence, forever at the limits of his resources, although this did to some extent depend upon his spending on relatively bourgeois luxuries, which he felt were necessities for his wife and children given their social status and the mores of the time. So the question comes was he paid to be a front man for the League of Just Men? Clearly he was advocating the overthrow of the system of nobility form which his wife came.

OLIVER CROMWELL

Figure 18: Oliver Cromwell

As was observed previously, every major change in history seems to have connected stories of robed figures moving in the background. In Oliver Cromwell's England, for instance, there has long been a story that prior to the late great battle that overthrew the monarchy Cromwell is supposed to have ordered a Major in his army to accompany him to a secret meeting. The meeting was in a grove of fog shrouded trees in a very desolated part of England. Sensing something out of the ordinary, his escort refused to go into the grove with Cromwell, so the future ruler of England went ahead on foot by himself.

The escort, though he did not advance with his leader, witnessed that Cromwell was met by a black robed figure that came out of the grove of trees. Remember, this was a place that for centuries had the reputation of being haunted, strange figures had been reported entering and leaving this grove. These stories about this area dated back to pagan times.

According to the story, this black robed figure is alleged to have given Cromwell a parchment that apparently sealed some agreement between them. Cromwell is reported to have exclaimed in anger that the parchment granted him far less time than they had bargained for. The black robed figure is supposed to have responded that the time period specified in the agreement was all the time Cromwell could be allowed. Apparently feeling that he had little choice, Cromwell accepted the agreement and the next day routed the King's forces. Then, according to the story, at the time specified as the end of the agreement in the parchment, Cromwell died. His dynasty died with him. A new king was returned to the throne of England.

NAPOLEON BONAPARTE

Figure 19: Napoleon

Napoleon was another world historical figure that came from very humble beginnings to reach the pinnacles of power. According to legend, Napoleon was supposed to have met with black robed figures in his royal palace. Though he was one of the most powerful men in the world, after each of these meetings he would be left shaken and scared. But, according to some sources, it was the advice that he received from these entities that allowed him to conquer all of Europe and threaten the rest of the world. It was allegedly his disobedience to their instructions that eventually led to his down fall. These mysterious figures appear to be hard task masters and historically they allow a pawn to disobey only once.

Interestingly, there was an interesting story that originated in Paris. Scientists were asked to conduct an investigation in regard to the remains of Napoleon[43]. According to the scientists examining the remains of Napoleon Bonaparte they were "deeply puzzled" by the discovery of a half-inch long

---

[43] Däniken, Eric Von, "Alien Chip In Napoleon's Skull", January 19, 2010, Weekly World News.

microchip embedded in Napoleon's skull. From its position and the conditions of the skull, this implant took place during his lifetime and the area of insertion had fully healed.

The researchers believe that this mysterious object could be an alien implant – suggesting that the French emperor was once abducted by a UFO!

"The possible ramifications of this discovery are almost too enormous to comprehend," declared Dr. Andre Dubois, who made the astonishing revelation in a French medical journal. *"Until now, every indication has been that victims of alien abduction are ordinary people who play no role in world events. Now we have compelling evidence that extraterrestrials acted in the past to influence human history – and may continue to do so!"*

Dr. Dubois made the amazing find while studying Napoleon's exhumed skeleton on a $140,000 grant from the French government. *"I was hoping to learn whether he suffered from a pituitary disorder that contributed to his small stature,"* he explained.

But instead the researcher found something far more extraordinary: *"As I examined the interior of the skull, my hand brushed across a tiny protrusion. I then looked at the area under a magnifying glass – and was stunned to find that the object was some kind of super-advanced microchip."*

From the extent of bone growth around the chip, the expert believes it was implanted when Bonaparte was young.

"Napoleon vanished from sight for a period of several days in July 1794, when he was 25. He later claimed he'd been held prisoner during the Themidorian coup – but no record of that arrest exists. I believe that is when the abduction took place." From that time on, Napoleon's rise was meteoric. By the next year, he'd been put in charge of the French army in Italy. Miraculously, he was able to transform starving, rag-tag troops into a top-notch fighting force and to crush the Italians.

In 1804, after a string of startling victories, the pint-size general crowned himself emperor of France – and his empire soon expanded to include what is now Germany and Austria, as well as Switzerland, Italy and Denmark.

"Napoleon used military strategies more than a hundred years ahead of his time," said Dr. Dubois. *"Perhaps the implant somehow enhanced his abilities."*

The implant could also explain Napoleon's famous habit of holding his hand over his heart. Dr. Dubois added.

"It's possible that the device affected the electrical signals from his brain to his heart."

By the time of his defeat by the British at Waterloo in 1815, Napoleon had altered the face of Europe.

"What Western history would have been like had the aliens not intervened, we can only guess," observed Dr. Dubois. *"Thus we cannot know whether they acted to help mankind or harm us."*

No one can argue that Napoleon Bonaparte did not have a major impact on world history. It would certainly explain a lot if it was confirmed that he was, in fact, implanted with a microchip, or some other way to control his acts.

ADOLF HITLER

Figure 20: Adolf Hitler

Adolf Hitler was another individual who came from obscurity to the heights of power. He was also a man who dreamed big and planned far in advance. Adolf Hitler put down his own funeral arrangements back in 1938 as he dreamt of the world domination he foresaw and his own personal worldwide glory. He wished to be laid to rest in the city of Lintz, in a giant burial vault of the National Socialist Party. A golden sepulcher decorated with gems from the Ural Mountains should have been installed in the center of the vault. The Russians reported that a badly charred corpse of Hitler was found in a bomb crater in the Imperial Chancellery's garden over 60 years ago. His mortal remains were reburied 8 times and eventually destroyed by fire. Of course that is only one story about what happened to Adolf Hitler. There are other stories that he was spirited out of Berlin during the last hours of the war by the same group of conspirators that had pushed Hitler to the very peak of power.

It is also interesting to note that in the ruins of Berlin, at the end of World War II, victorious Russian troops found the bodies of a number of black robed figures[44]. The general descriptions led people reading the reports to speculate that these were the bodies of the Oriental monks who were said to have come to Berlin from the Far East. However, another view would be that these descriptions also fit the descriptions of the so-called Men In Black that plague witness to UFO sightings.

It is known that Hitler was another in a long list of former world leaders who believed implicitly in the existence of a "Master Race". Modern research is continually turning up new areas of the occult that were practiced or the subject of research by the "mighty Third Reich". There is much evidence that Hitler had contact with strange figures in black robes. In fact, many nights he would wake up screaming that one of the "Masters" had come to visit him. He always described them as wearing black robes.

Hitler victimized an entire continent and exterminated millions in his quest to create a so-called "Master Race." The world thought Hitler was mad and barely understood his rationales, but actually, the concept of a white, blond-haired, blue-eyed master Nordic race did not originate with Adolf Hitler. The idea that there was actually a so called Master Race was really created in the United States at least two decades before Hitler came to power. It was the product of the American eugenics movement.

EUGENICS

Eugenics is the study and practice of selective breeding applied to humans, with the aim of improving the species. In a historical and broader sense, eugenics can also be a study of "improving human genetic qualities Eugenics is the study and practice of selective breeding applied to humans, with the aim of improving the species. It was a racist American pseudoscience designed to wipe out all human beings except those who conformed to a predetermined stereotype. This philosophy was enshrined into national policy through forced sterilization of those who did not meet

---

[44] Pauwels, Louis and Jacques Bergier, THE MORNING OF THE MAGICIANS, Stein and Day, New York. 1960.

the desired stereotype, segregation laws and marriage restrictions that were enacted in 27 states.

Ultimately, the powers behind the eugenics movement championed laws that were passed that coercively sterilized some 60,000 Americans, barred the marriage of thousands, forcibly segregated thousands more in colonies and persecuted untold numbers in ways we are still just learning. Only after eugenics and race biology became firmly entrenched as an American ideal was the campaign transplanted to Germany, where it came to Hitler's attention.

Figure 21L Eugenics Info.

According to records left by the Third Reich, Hitler studied American eugenic laws and rationales and sought to legitimize his innate race hatred and anti-Semitism by medicalizing it and wrapping it in a pseudoscientific facade. Indeed, Hitler was able to attract many reasonable Germans to his movement by claiming that science was on his side. While Hitler's race hatred certainly sprung from his own mind, the intellectual outlines of the eugenics methods that Hitler adopted in 1924 were strictly American.

Eugenics would have been little more than bizarre parlor talk had it not been for massive financing by corporate philanthropies, specifically the Carnegie Institution, the Rockefeller Foundation and the Harriman railroad fortune. These prestigious and wealthy organizations were in league with America's most respected scientists from prestigious universities such as Harvard, Yale and Princeton. These academicians, for all of the best reasons, faked and twisted existing scientific data to serve eugenics' racist aims.

It is also interesting to note that the Rockefeller, Harriman and Carnegie families have been at the center of the conspiracy theories of tens of thousands of researchers. In fact, many of the most blatant actions that have worked to undermine the sovereignty of the nation as well as the rights of its citizens have been financially underwritten by these same families. SO why would they work to undermine the very system that has given them their unbelievably wealth.

In fact it was the Carnegie Institution that effectively invented the American Eugenics movement when it established a laboratory complex at Cold Spring Harbor, on Long Island dedicated to the study of Eugenics. This complex stockpiled millions of index cards on ordinary Americans as the movement carefully plotted the removal of entire families, certain bloodlines[45] and whole peoples from the face of the earth. From Cold Spring Harbor, eugenics advocates agitated in the state legislatures of America as well as in the nation's social service agencies and associations.

The Harriman railroad fortune paid local charities, such as the New York Bureau of Industries and Immigration, to seek out Jewish, Italian and other immigrants in New York and other crowded cities and subject them to deportation, confinement or forced sterilization.

The Rockefeller Foundation helped found and fund the German eugenics program, and it even single handedly funded the program that ultimately sent SS physician Josef Mengele[46] into Auschwitz where he conducted his infamous study of twins.

The Rockefeller Foundation, the Carnegie Institution, Cold Spring Harbor Laboratory and the Max Planck Institute — the successor to the Kaiser Wilhelm Institute — all gave unlimited access and unstinting assistance in the course of this investigation into creation of the Master Race. Though it was American interests who gave this pseudoscience its greatest push, long before the advent of America's leading philanthropies, however, eugenics was born as a scientific curiosity in the Victorian age.

---

[45] This is certainly in keeping with the idea that there has been an eons long war between warring factions within the "gods". Wipe out the bloodline, end the opposition.

[46] Josef Mengele who was born 16 March 1911 and died, perhaps, on 7 February 1979 is also known as the Angel of Death. He was a German SS officer and a physician in the Nazi concentration camp Auschwitz-Burkina. He earned doctorates in anthropology from Munich University and in medicine from Frankfurt University. He initially gained notoriety for being one of the SS physicians who supervised the selection of arriving transports of prisoners, determining who was to be killed and who was to become a forced laborer, but he became far more infamous for performing grisly human experiments on camp inmates, for which Mengele was called the "Angel of Death".

In 1863, Sir Francis Galton, a cousin of Charles Darwin, theorized that if talented people married only other talented people, the result would be measurably better offspring. At the turn of the last century, Galton's ideas were imported into the United States just about the time that Gregor Mendel[47]'s principles of heredity were rediscovered. American eugenic advocates believed with religious fervor that Mendelian concepts explaining the color and size of peas, corn and cattle also governed the social and intellectual character of man.

In the early twentieth century, America was continually reeling from the upheaval of massive immigration and was also still torn by post-Reconstruction chaos. Race conflict was everywhere.

Elitists, utopians and so-called progressives fused their smoldering race fears and class bias with their desire to make a better world, reinventing Galton's eugenics as a repressive and racist ideology. Their intent was to populate the earth with vastly more of their own socioeconomic and biological kind, and less or none of everyone else.

The superior species the eugenics movement sought was not merely tall, strong and talented; eugenicists craved blond, blue-eyed Nordic types. This group alone, they believed, was fit to inherit the earth. Many researchers believe that this was the original appearance of the "gods" of antiquity. Thus this bizarre area of the scientific fringe was actually an attempt to "purify" the race, the very thing Hitler stove to do. This would tend to support the idea that the "gods" are still with us, trying to weed the race.

In the process of purifying the race, the movement intended to subtract blacks, Indians, Hispanics, Eastern Europeans, Jews, dark-haired hill folk, poor people, the infirm — essentially, anyone outside the gentrified genetic lines drawn up by American raceologists. IN doing so, it

---

[47] Gregor Johann Mendel was born July 20, 1822 and died January 6, 1884 was an Augustinian priest and scientist, who gained posthumous fame as the figurehead of the new science of genetics for his study of the inheritance of certain traits in pea plants. Mendel showed that the inheritance of these traits follows particular laws, which were later named after him. The significance of Mendel's work was not recognized until the turn of the 20th century. The independent rediscovery of these laws formed the foundation of the modern science of genetics.

would reduce the amount of humans on the planet to a manageable number and leave on those of "pure" blood.

How would they do it? By identifying so-called "defective" family trees and subjecting them to lifelong segregation and sterilization programs designed to kill their bloodlines. The grand plan was literally to wipe away the reproductive capability of the "unfit" — those deemed weak and inferior.

Eighteen solutions were explored in a Carnegie-supported study in 1911 called *"Preliminary Report of the Committee of the Eugenic Section of the American Breeder's Association to Study and to Report on the Best Practical Means for Cutting Off the Defective Germ-Plasm in the Human Population."*

Figure 22: Justice Oliver Wendell Holmes

Although the eighth of the eighteen solutions was euthanasia, the leaders of the movement believed it was too early to implement this solution. Instead, the main solution was the rapid expansion of forced segregation and sterilization, as well as increased marriage restrictions. The most commonly suggested method of eugenicide in America was a "lethal chamber," or gas chamber. The forerunner of Hitler's final solution.

The reader might think that such activities would be quickly outlawed in the land of the free and the home of the brave. However, even the United States Supreme Court, the highest law in the land, endorsed eugenics as national policy. In a 1927 decision, Buck v. Bell[48], no less a voice of reason than Supreme Court Justice Oliver Wendell Holmes[49] wrote, *"It is better for all*

---

[48] Buck v. Bell, 274 U.S. 200 (1927)
[49] Oliver Wendell Holmes, Jr. was born March 8, 1841 and died March 6, 1935. He was an American jurist who served as an associate justice on the Supreme Court of the United States from 1902 to 1932. Noted for his long service, his concise and pithy opinions, and

the world, if instead of waiting to execute degenerate offspring for crime, or to let them starve for their imbecility, society can prevent those who are manifestly unfit from continuing their kind . . . Three generations of imbeciles are enough."

Ironically, years later, the Nazis quoted Holmes' words in their own defense at the Nuremberg trials.

During the 1920s, Carnegie Institution eugenics scientists cultivated deep personal and professional relationships with Germany's fascist eugenicists. In fact their teachings were so wide spread in Germany that in 1924, when Hitler wrote "Mein Kampf[50]," he frequently quoted American eugenic ideology and openly displayed a thorough knowledge of American eugenics and its phraseology.

"There is today one state," Hitler wrote, *"in which at least weak beginnings toward a better conception* [of immigration] *are noticeable. Of course, it is not our model German Republic, but the United States."*

Hitler proudly told his comrades just how closely he followed American eugenic legislation in the planning for his own Final Solution.

"I have studied with great interest the laws of several American states concerning prevention of reproduction by people whose progeny would, in all probability, be of no value or be injurious to the racial stock," he told a fellow Nazi.

Hitler even wrote a fan letter to American eugenic leader Madison Grant[51], calling his race-based eugenics book, "The Passing of the Great

---

his deference to the decisions of elected legislatures, he is one of the most widely cited United States Supreme Court justices in history, particularly for his "clear and present danger" majority opinion in the 1919 case of Schenck v. United States, and is one of the most influential American common-law judges.

[50] Volume 1 of Mein Kampf was published in 1925 and Volume 2 in 1926. The book was edited by Jesuit priest Bernard Staempfle who later perished during the Night of the Long Knives. Mein Kampf ("My Struggle"), Jackie (originally 1925–1926), Reissue edition (September 15, 1998), Publisher: Mariner Books, Language: English, paperback, 720 pages, ISBN 0-395-92503-7

[51] Madison Grant was an American lawyer, historian and physical anthropologist, known primarily for his work as a eugenicist and conservationist. As a eugenicist, Grant was responsible for one of the most famous works of scientific racism, and played an active role in crafting strong immigration restriction and anti-miscegenation laws in the United States.

Race[52]," his "bible." Hitler's deputy, Rudolf Hess, coined a popular adage in the Reich: "National Socialism is nothing but applied biology."

Hitler's struggle for a superior race became a mad crusade for a Master Race, exchanging the American term "Nordic" for "Germanic" or "Aryan." Race science, racial purity and racial dominance became the driving force behind Hitler's Nazism. Nazi eugenics ultimately would dictate who would be persecuted in a Reich-dominated Europe, how people would live and how they would die.

Nazi doctors would become the unseen generals in Hitler's war against the Jews and other Europeans deemed inferior. Doctors would create the science, devise the eugenic formulas, and even hand-select the victims for sterilization, euthanasia and mass extermination.

During the Third Reich's first decade, eugenicists across America welcomed Hitler's plans as the logical fulfillment of their own decades of research and effort. Ten years after Virginia passed its 1924 sterilization act, Joseph DeJarnette, superintendent of Virginia's Western State Hospital, complained in the Richmond Times-Dispatch, *"The Germans are beating us at our own game."* In 1934, sterilizations of "undesirables" in Germany were accelerating beyond 5,000 per month.

Returning from a visit to Germany, the California eugenics leader C. M. Goethe bragged to a key colleague, *"You will be interested to know, that your work has played a powerful part in shaping the opinions of the group of intellectuals who are behind Hitler in this epoch-making program. Everywhere I sensed that their opinions have been tremendously stimulated by American thought . . . I want you, my dear friend, to carry this thought with you for the rest of your life, that you have really jolted into action a great government of 60 million people."*

Beyond the scientific road map, America used its money to fund and help found Germany's eugenic institutions. By 1926, Rockefeller had

---

[52] The Passing of The Great Race; or, The racial basis of European history was an influential book of scientific racism written by the American eugenicist, lawyer, and amateur anthropologist Madison Grant in 1916. Grant, Madison (1921). The Passing of the Great Race (4 ed.). C. Scribner's sons. p. 167.

donated some $410,000 — an amount equal to almost $4 million in today's dollars — to hundreds of German researchers.

In May 1926, for example, Rockefeller awarded $250,000 to the German Psychiatric Institute of the Kaiser Wilhelm Institute, which became the Kaiser Wilhelm Institute for Psychiatry. Among the leading psychiatrists at the German Psychiatric Institute was Ernst Rudin, who became director and eventually an architect of Hitler's systematic medical repression.

Another in the Kaiser Wilhelm Institute's complex of eugenic institutions was the Institute for Brain Research. Since 1915, it had operated out of a single room, but everything changed when Rockefeller money arrived in 1929.

A grant of $317,000 allowed the institute to construct a major building and take center stage in German race biology. The Institute for Brain Research received additional grants from the Rockefeller Foundation during the next several years.

Leading the Brain institute was — once again — Hitler's medical henchman Ernst Rudin. Rudin's organization became a prime director and recipient of murderous experimentation and research conducted on Jews, Gypsies and others.

Beginning in 1940, in addition to the "lesser races, thousands of Germans taken from old age homes, mental institutions and other custodial facilities were systematically gassed. In all, between 50,000 and 100,000 Germans were killed.

"*While we were pussy-footing around,*" said Leon Whitney, executive secretary of the American Eugenics Society, "*the Germans were calling a spade a spade.*"

A special recipient of Rockefeller funding was the Kaiser Wilhelm Institute for Anthropology, Human Heredity and Eugenics in Berlin. For decades, American eugenicists had craved twins to advance their research into heredity. The institute was now prepared to undertake such research on an unprecedented level.

On May 13, 1932, the Rockefeller Foundation in New York dispatched a radiogram to its Paris office that read: "*JUNE MEETING*

EXECUTIVE COMMITTEE NINE THOUSAND DOLLARS OVER THREE YEAR PERIOD TO KWG INSTITUTE ANTHROPOLOGY FOR RESEARCH ON TWINS AND EFFECTS ON LATER GENERATIONS OF SUBSTANCES TOXIC FOR GERM PLASM."

At the time of Rockefeller's endowment, Otmar Freiherr von Verschuer, a hero in American eugenics circles, functioned as a head of the Institute for Anthropology, Human Heredity and Eugenics. Rockefeller funding of the Institute for Anthropology continued directly and through other research conduits during Verschuer's early tenure.

In 1935, Verschuer left the Institute to form a rival eugenic facility in Frankfurt that was much heralded in the American eugenic press.

Research on twins in the Third Reich exploded, backed up by government decrees mobilizing all twins. At about that time, Verschuer wrote in *Der Erbarzt*, a eugenic doctors' journal he edited, that Germany's war would yield a "total solution to the Jewish problem."

JOSEF MENGELE

Verschuer had a long-time assistant. His name was Josef Mengele. On May 30, 1943, Mengele arrived at Auschwitz. Verschuer notified the German Research Society, "My assistant, Dr. Josef Mengele (M.D., Ph.D.) joined me in this branch of research. He is presently employed as Hauptsturmfuhrer [captain] and camp physician in the Auschwitz concentration camp. Anthropological testing of the most diverse racial groups in this concentration camp is being carried out with permission of the SS Reichsfuhrer [Heinrich Himmler]."

Figure 23: Josef Mengele

Mengele began searching boxcars that arrived at the camp for twins. When he found them, he performed beastly experiments, scrupulously wrote up the reports and sent the paperwork back to Verschuer's institute for evaluation.

Often, cadavers, eyes and other body parts also were dispatched to Berlin's other eugenic institutes.

Rockefeller executives never knew of Mengele, or at least they never admitted that they did. . With few exceptions, the foundation had ceased all eugenic studies in Nazi-occupied Europe before World War II erupted in 1939. But by that time the die had been cast.

The talented men Rockefeller and Carnegie had financed, the great institutions they helped found and the science they helped create took on a scientific momentum of their own.

What stopped the race biologists of Berlin, Munich and Auschwitz?

Certainly, the Nazis felt they were unstoppable; they imagined a thousand-year Reich of super bred men.

But something did vanquish Mengele and his colleagues. On June 6, 1944, the Allies invaded at Normandy and began defeating the Nazis, town by town and often street by street. They closed in on Germany from the west, while the Soviet army overran the Auschwitz death camp from the east on Jan. 27, 1945. Mengele fled.

Auschwitz was indeed the last stand of eugenics. The science of the strong almost completely prevailed in its war against the weak. Almost. Edwin Black is the New York Times bestselling author of the award-winning "IBM and the Holocaust" and the just-released "War Against the Weak" ("Four Walls Eight Windows"), from which this article is adapted. He can be reached via www.edwinblack.com.

THOMAS JEFFERSON

Late one night in 1783, Thomas Jefferson was out walking in his garden, contemplating the design for a national emblem for the United States. According to the story, he suddenly found himself face to face with a swarthy complexioned individual of medium height, wearing a long dark cape[53] (Sound familiar?). This strange visitor handed Jefferson a parchment

---

[53] Allen, Gary and Larry Abraham, NONE DARE CALL IT CONSPIRACY, Double A Publications, Suite 403, 18000 Highway South, Seattle, Washington 98188.

upon which was depicted the design for the Great Seal. This design was later accepted by the Continental Congress.

It should be pointed out that Thomas Jefferson was reputed to be a member of the Order of the Bees, an affiliated branch of the Illuminati. The same Illuminati that in the guise of the League of Just Men paid Karl Marx to publish the Communist Manifesto. Interesting that a founding member of our own government would be a member of an organization that wanted to unite the world under one government and appears to have given birth to the Communist Manifesto[54].

Figure 24: Thomas Jefferson

Thomas Jefferson was the third president of the United States, serving from 1801 to 1809. He was confirmed as a member of the Masons in spite of the poor records kept by the Colonial Lodges and the destruction of records by fire and war. In a number of instances this makes it impossible to consult original Lodge records. Jefferson may have been a Member of Charlottesville Lodge No. 90, Charlottesville, Va., since his name appears on the Minutes of this Lodge on September 20, 1817.

Jefferson was also a member of the Lodge of the Nine Muses in Paris and the Beenan Order (Order of the Bees) known outside Bavaria as the Illuminati. Jefferson's Vice President, from 1801 to 1805, Aaron Burr, was also a confirmed Mason. What was even more interesting is the fact the Burr was also a member of the Collins family of Satanists who called themselves the Hell Fire Club. Thomas Jefferson was one of the members of this purely Satanic group who practiced satanic sexual occult rituals[55].

---

54 Ibid.

[55]Springmeier, Fritz, The Illuminati Bloodlines.

Jefferson's second vice president from 1805 to 1809 was George Clinton, another confirmed Mason and also a member of the Illuminati[56].

OUTSIDE INFLUENCES

After looking at the information presented above, there can be little doubt that there has been a massive effort to purify the race through scientific methods. What is the most telling in a study of this movement is that the impetus for the imposition of methods that we could call barbaric actually came from some of the most prominent families and institutions in this country. It is also interesting to note that the stereotype for the Master Race is actually the blonde Nordic type which is so closely associated with occupants of UFOs. Most of this involved in the Eugenics movement were not of this Aryan movement. This does raise the question as to why someone would support a movement that would ultimately be used against their own self-interest. Thus is puzzling to say the least.

---

[56] http://www.city-data.com/forum/religion-philosophy/141314-order-eastern-star-free-mason-12.html#ixzz0oOqYotdG

CHAPTER SIX
DE'JA'VU ALL OVER AGAIN

This chapter is going to raise some interesting and startling issues. Here we are going to talk about black operations and black science, two terms that have come to have special meaning to many people. Unfortunately, the majority of people worldwide do not know what the terms Black Operations and Black Sciences mean or how they are used. Most think, if they are even aware of the eugenics program that led to Hitler's accesses, that such programs are dead. However, that is not true. So let us step behind the curtain and take a peek at some of the ongoing programs today.

BLACK OPERATIONS

A black operation or black op is a covert operation typically involving activities that are highly clandestine and, often, outside of standard military protocol. Black Operations were widely thought to have developed in the years immediately after World War I, but really flourished after World War II during the Cold War. Really anything that military or government leaders wanted to undertake but did not want the voters to know about was dubbed a black operation.

Congress allocated money to the Pentagon, the C.I.A. and other Defense Department sectors to make the United States military as strong as possible, but certain projects were considered to be more secretive than others. The more secret projects were funded by certain select members of the civilian sector at first, most funded by defense contractors already in the loop.

As time went on, those privy to the many secret projects developed into a real clique of not only specially screened corporations, but also choice individuals found by federal talent hunts. A new sub-culture was born with a new personality and belief system, completely cut off from mainstream Americans. It was in this new belief system that many of the more bizarre programs found enthusiastic backers.

Cutting-edge technology such as the stealth aircraft, invisible hover-craft, extremely low frequency mind control (E.L.F.) and weather control, in addition to the cloning or reproduction of identical species, became referred to as "Secret Sciences'. This new knowledge wasn't, and in many respects still is not, available to the regular Army, to Congress, or to any University. The most secret of the many secrets were in the hands of a power hungry few that tied itself to the World Bank for the future funding of its projects. They developed "think-tanks' like Stanford Research Institute and Tavistock to keep the masses fooled about virtually everything that was being worked on behind the tightly closed doors of government research. However, many of these new sciences were actually rehashes of older ideas.

The use of deception to keep out those not in the accepted leadership group grew like a cancer into every area of industrialized society. These new members of the elite moved into everything - from the Mafia, to Harvard University, to International Banking. This group of ultimate insiders learned how to control the media, and thus, they controlled television, Hollywood, every newspaper, every educational institution and every person's mind, at least to a certain point.

This included operating behind the scenes in regard to many government agencies. These insiders caused many problems in world events. In fact, the carrying out of the desires of these insiders has often led to the violation of basic human rights. In fact these actions on the part of federal agents led to accusations of abuse and inhuman acts by the C.I.A. and F.B.I. were investigated by Congress in 1977. These agencies used the excuse of "national security" for every crime they committed.

Hidden under the blanket of "national security' there has not been an investigation of their highly illegal activities since 1977. There is much evidence that Congress, the President and even the U.S. Supreme Court are actually scared of these ultimate insiders. A mountain of evidence points to the fact that they have killed thousands, including corporate executives and politicians - perhaps they were behind the assassination of JFK. Thus, this group of select insiders are considered the "Invisible Government"!

THE INVISIBLE GOVERNMENT

So the first question is what is the invisible government? Well in actuality, there are two governments in the United States today. One is visible. The other is invisible, but incredibly powerful none the less.

The first is the government that citizens read about in their newspapers and children study about in their civics books. The visible government is the one that is allegedly of the people, by the people and for the people. The second is the interlocking, hidden machinery that carries out the policies of the United States.

This second, invisible government gathers intelligence, conducts espionage, and plans and executes secret operations all over the globe. The Invisible Government is not a formal body in the sense that there is no formal overlord. It is a loose, amorphous grouping of individuals and agencies drawn from many parts of the visible government. It is not limited to the Central Intelligence Agency, although the CIA is at its heart. Nor is it confined to the nine other agencies which comprise what is known as the intelligence community:

- National Security Council
- Defense Intelligence Agency
- National Security Agency
- Army Intelligence
- Navy Intelligence
- Air Force Intelligence
- State Department's Bureau of Intelligence and Research
- Atomic Energy Commission
- Federal Bureau of Investigation

The Invisible Government includes, also, many other units and agencies, as well as individuals, that appear outwardly to be a normal part of the conventional government. It even encompasses business firms and institutions that are seemingly private.

To an extent that is only beginning to be perceived, this shadow government is shaping the lives of over 300,000,000 Americans. Major decisions involving peace or war are actually taking place out of public view. An informed citizen might come to suspect that the foreign policy of the United States often works publicly in one direction and secretly through the Invisible Government in just the opposite direction.

This Invisible Government is not a relatively new institution. Though it may be much older, appears to have come into being as a result of two related factors: the rise of the United States as a power after the War of 1812 and the continued challenge to that power by the British government. The power of this invisible government was increased after World War II when the United States rose to a position of pre-eminent world power, and then was challenged by Soviet Communism.

After World War II the invisible government was reorganized into a more cohesive team through a Continuity of Operations Plan (or Continuity of Government Plan) which has been a part of government operations since at least the Cold War, when President Dwight D. Eisenhower provided (via executive order) various measures designed to ensure that the government of the United States would be able to continue operating after a nuclear war.

These plans were classified for many years, partly under the assumption that knowledge of these plans would enable the Soviet Union to more effectively launch a nuclear attack. In addition, these plans were censored to prevent an uproar among the American public, who (proponents feared) might panic after the revelation that the government was planning for its own survival in a terrifying post-nuclear war environment. With the fall of the Berlin Wall, these plans lost their prominence both in government and in the public consciousness. The Continuity of Operations Plan has seen a return to relevance in the 2000s.

After the September 11 attacks, many speculated that terrorists might attempt to destroy a large part of the central government and send the country into chaos. Much of the government's plans for post-nuclear war survival remain secret, and some of the measures that are known are controversial.

These measures included construction of underground facilities such as "Mount Weather", a hollowed-out putatively nuclear-proof mountain in western Virginia with a mailing address in Berryville, Virginia. The public can now tour one such facility, intended to house the entire United States Congress, on the grounds of the Greenbrier Resort in White Sulphur Springs, West Virginia. Other provisions of the plans included executive orders that designated certain government officials to assume Cabinet and other executive branch positions and carry out the responsibilities of the position if the primary office holders are killed. There has been a formal line of succession to the presidency since 1792 (currently found in the Presidential Succession Act of 1947, 3 U.S.C. § 19). This runs from the Vice President to the Speaker of the House of Representatives, President pro tempore of the Senate, and then through the Cabinet secretaries in a sequence specified by Congress.

It was a much graver challenge than any which had previously confronted the Republic. The Soviet world strategy threatened the very survival of the nation. It employed an espionage network that was dedicated to the subversion of the power and ideals of the United States. To meet that challenge the United States began constructing a vast intelligence and espionage system of its own. This has mushroomed to extraordinary proportions out of public view and quite apart from the traditional political process.

By 1964 the intelligence network had grown into a massive, hidden apparatus, at that time secretly employing about 200,000 persons and spending several billion dollars a year.

"*The National Security Act of 1947*," in the words of Allen W. Dulles, "*has given Intelligence a more influential position in our government than Intelligence enjoys in any other government of the world.*"

Because of its massive size and pervasive secrecy, the Invisible Government became the inevitable target of suspicion and criticism. It has been accused by some knowledgeable congressmen and other influential citizens, including a former President, Harry S. Truman, of conducting a foreign policy of its own, and of meddling deeply in the affairs of other countries without presidential authority.

The American people have not been in a position to assess these charges. They know virtually nothing about the Invisible Government. Its employment rolls are classified. Its activities are top- secret. Its budget is concealed in other appropriations. Congress provides money for the Invisible Government without knowing how much it has appropriated or how it will be spent. A handful of congressmen are supposed to be kept informed by the Invisible Government, but they know relatively little about how it works.

Overseas, in foreign capitals, American ambassadors are supposed to act as the supreme civilian representatives of the President of the United States. They are told they have control over the agents of the Invisible Government. But do they? The agents maintain communications and codes of their own. And the ambassador's authority has been judged by a committee of the United States Senate to be a "polite fiction."

At home, the intelligence men are directed by law to leave matters to the FBI. But the CIA maintains more than a score of offices in major cities throughout the United States; it is deeply involved in many domestic activities, from broadcasting stations and a steamship company to the university campus.

The Invisible Government is also generally thought to be under the direct control of the National Security Council. But, in fact, many of its major decisions are never discussed in the Council. These decisions are handled by a small directorate, the name of which is only whispered. How many Americans have ever heard of the "Special Group"? (Also known as the "54/12 Group.") The name of this group, even its existence, is unknown outside the innermost circle of the Invisible Government.

The Vice-President is by law a member of the National Security Council, but he does not participate in the discussions of the Special

Group. As Vice-President, Lyndon B. Johnson was privy to more government secrets than any of his predecessors. But he was not truly involved with the Invisible Government until he was sworn in as the thirty-sixth President of the United States.

On November 23, 1963, during the first hour of his first full day in office, Johnson was taken by McGeorge Bundy -- who had been President Kennedy's personal link with the Special Group -- to the Situation Room, a restricted command post deep in the White House basement.

There, surrounded by top-secret maps, electronic equipment and communications outlets, the new President was briefed by the head of the Invisible Government, John Alex McCone[57], Director of Central Intelligence and a member of the Special Group. Although Johnson knew the men who ran the Invisible Government and was aware of much of its workings, it was not until that morning that he began to see the full scope of its organization and secrets.

In the harsh conditions of the mid-twentieth century, the nation's leaders have increasingly come to feel that certain decisions must be made by them alone without popular consent, and in secret, if the nation is to survive. The area of this secret decision-making has grown rapidly, and the size of the Invisible Government has increased proportionately.

To what extent is this secret government compatible with the American system, or necessary to preserve it? Will it gradually change the character of the institutions it seeks to preserve? If the American people are to try to answer these questions they must first achieve a greater level of understanding about the secret government itself.

"I know no safe depository of the ultimate powers of the society but the people themselves," said Thomas Jefferson, "and if we think them not enlightened enough to exercise their control with a wholesome discretion, the remedy is not to take it from them, but to inform their discretion."

---

[57]On April 11, 1965, President Johnson replaced McCone with retired Vice-Admiral William F. Raborn, who served only 14 months as CIA director and was in turn replaced, on June 18, 1966, by Deputy Director Richard M. Helms, a career CIA operator.

This book is an effort to thus inform the American people that there is a secret society operating behind the scene staffed and operated by some of the most powerful people in this nation. For beyond the mere gathering of intelligence, the secret government has engaged in "special operations," ranging from political warfare to paramilitary activities and full-scale invasion.

Under certain conditions, and on a limited, controlled basis, such special operations may sometimes prove necessary. But they cannot become so unwieldy that they are irreconcilable with the kind of society that has launched them. When that happens, the result is disaster. This was nowhere better illustrated than on the beaches of Cuba.

The invisible government became an internationally funded and operated organization that developed its totalitarian tactics for worldwide economic, political and military control. Through its various outlets, the invisible government has led us to believe that half of the earth was religious-capitalism, defended by the CIA and the other half of the world was atheist-communist, defended by the KGB.

But, in actuality, the International Bankers and ancient esoteric secret societies - with an octopus of intelligence agencies - controlled the entire earth, even though World Wars I and II. Whenever a few cliques decided to go into business for themselves and break away from the monopoly system, we would have a world war. The same is true today, so be forewarned; do not mess with the super bankers!

The Cold War ended because of a worldwide cry for "peace". The old industrialist/banker game of churning up yet another war for the military/industrial complex was becoming more and more difficult. Their "think tanks" had to come up with a new strategy to subdue this "New Left" ideology.

Time also changed technology, thus the bankers and industrialists no longer needed large populations to do the farming, work in the factories or even fight in their war-machine game. Advanced computers, robots and artificial intelligence, bio-electronics and cloning eliminated the need of all of these "useless eaters'. Top secret meetings were held and a strategy initiated (as early as 1960). One such example is found in "The Report from Iron Mountain".

REPORT FROM IRON MOUNTAIN

The "New Left," with all of its altruistic and humanitarian concepts, would be the "Trojan Horse" that would bring in the largest shadow of death to fall on mankind in the written history of the earth. "Globalist" books reveal the hidden agenda behind the United Nations, the covert meanings of their statues and art at the new Masonic airports, and their shrines like the Georgia Guide Stones. All of these items call for a massive depopulation of the earth!

They also propose the elimination of democracy and culture, under the guise of a new positive program devised by one of their "think-tanks'. The Proposed Agenda – A one-world religion, a one-world government - In other words, a New World Order. How many times have we had that repetitive phrase thrust into our faces?

On the other hand, certain racist "New Right' organizations have been, and are currently, manipulated by the Black Ops agent provocateurs. Their motivation is to make these groups appear hostile to the masses through their "Song Bird' media. The truth is that these groups are very aware of certain concepts of the New World Order, but, they cannot see that they being used as "scapegoats and patsies" for Black Operations' sabotage. The invisible government always uses some sort of instigated chaos to steer public demand for social change. Gun control is a perfect example of this!

Their hoodwinking games are from the old Masonic term, "Ordo Abo Chao." They covertly create the problem, but their politicians come forward publicly with the perfect solution: Order Out of Chaos.

The Invisible Government's old mantra was national security, its excuse for cruelty to mankind. Now, there are a whole string of pacifications like: "To save the children" or "To save nature!"

The truth is that the invisible government is destroying more nature with its top secret projects like the nuclear bomb, chemical and biological warfare and HAARP (High-Frequency Active Auroral Research Program), than we, the "useless eaters,' could ever imagine doing.

When the Berlin wall came down, the Black Operations of the East merged with the Black Operations of the West. The "think tanks' now include the Soviets and Red Chinese. They have mixed their ideas for a One World Order with military Special Forces; this combination in scheming collusion in order to execute their "cleansing or killing field" immoral programs.

What these Brave New World types do not know is that, once again, they are being used to satisfy the greedy appetites of the Super Power Elite. Those in the inner circle know that an inter-dimensional society, an etheric civilization more invisible than they are, control their minds and souls. They honor these Ascended Masters or Gods with blood and sacrifice, as they always have, through their history of the Dark Nobility and Black Arts Occultism. These gods that they worship are actually the ancient gods of pre-history who today are referred to as the Annunaki.

The "Black Budget" then started to be used for the "Black Arts" and became known as the Black Sciences. The earliest projects actually started prior to World War I, while the more popular ones started around World War II. The U.S. Army's Manhattan Project was in charge of making the A-bomb, while U.S. Navy dealt with Stealth equipment and invisibility, as evidenced in the Philadelphia Experiment After the war, the scientists of both projects were joined with Nazi scientists from Germany and NASA.

From this merging, the National Security Agency was officially inaugurated. Previous experiments like "Babylon-Working[58]' and the "Montauk Project[59]" were started using Nazi occultists and scientists to

---

[58] The Babylon Working was a series of magic ceremonies or rituals commenced on March 2, 1946 by author, pioneer rocket-fuel scientist, and occultist Jack Parsons, essentially designed to manifest an individual incarnation of the archetypal divine feminine called Babylon, as well as to catalyze the emergence of that force in society and as it exists latently in every man and woman.

[59] The Montauk Project was alleged to be a series of secret United States government projects conducted at Camp Hero or Montauk Air Force Station on Montauk, Long Island

communicate with and materialize inter-dimensional beings. They were the "unofficial' pioneers of projects working on inter-dimensional time travel and eugenics/cloning. Thus, with these projects, The Black Sciences were officially, yet covertly born. In spite of the laughter with which the suggest is met, there is little question that there is a segment of the covert community that believes strongly in the power of magic.

Black Sciences, the science of the impossible; the very concept smacks very strongly of the most far out science fiction. Disbelief is the common reaction to any discussion of such things. How is it possible? Does magic really exist.

Most people can't escape their erroneous intuitive sense of the world as they think it may be. Most believe that mathematics is the language of truth. However, there is another dimension of math. As Richard Feynman said, "if you aren't deeply disturbed by quantum mechanics, you clearly haven't understood it."

They theory of Relativity is inconceivable to most as a truth about the laws of time and space in our universe. Similarly people will have difficulties with superconductor Josephine sensors measuring a single quantum of energy or that your mental experiences are completely contained in the electrical properties of the brain.

Deciphering the brain code has been a primary research direction, the Holy Grail, for most neural scientists. And they are getting very close in the civilian world to completely deciphering it. However, the very idea that there was a code to the human brain is a concept that is staggering to consider and even more mind blowing that this code and be understood by the mind of man.

To help the skeptical readers open their minds to unbelievable scientific realities, let me illustrate some well documented feats of science. Would you have believed someone who said that a ball weighing a kilogram of an element could destroy an entire city before the nuclear bomb was demonstrated? If someone told you that a several ton metal tube

---

for the purpose of developing psychological warfare techniques and exotic research including time travel. Jacques Vallée describes allegations of the Montauk Project as an outgrowth of stories about the Philadelphia Experiment.

could lift itself 30,000 feet above sea level on its own propulsion before airplanes became common, would you have believed them? Would you believe someone who claimed that they could view individual atoms, if you hadn't heard of an electron tunneling microscope? If NASA didn't post images of quasars near the edge of the known universe, would you believe that one could see 9 billion light years away (53 trillion miles away).

Some people are still in disbelief that humans have walked on the moon. Many people use mobile phones but have no idea how they work. Golf ball sized objects are tracked from the ground in space orbit. Amateur microwave enthusiasts have bounced microwaves off the moon back to Earth (called Earth Moon Earth, EME). Even teleportation technology is working at a quantum scale with a phenomenon called quantum entanglement.

Scientific breakthroughs are always met with skepticism before the majority of the population has been exposed to the breakthrough. Wireless EEG cloning/heterodyning has been around for 30+ years but the selfishness and stupidity of the scientists and military figures involved for not seeing a more important global beneficial optima for releasing this technology for medical, commercial, and other uses has stymied and hindered the collective intelligence of the population from developing it. It is currently

The Black Sciences are the "Most Secret of all Secrets" and are said to be seriously guarded by special, screened soldiers, trained and born out of covert, Black Operations groups. It is this elitist group's steadfast hope to merge the seen world with the unseen world. Their prioritized goal is currently designed to ensure that the world has a "oneness-of mind" (the hive concept), in addition to being spiritually harmonized to a designated frequency that will bring their plan into full activation. The "Ascended Masters" have commanded them to eliminate the Old World, with its old ideas, old way of thinking and all of its old people.

A new generation with a "New World View" is the agenda of the day. That is why many conservatives, Christians, Jews, Muslims, Buddhists, etc. are on the surveillance and extermination lists. That is why more anti-Constitutional laws are becoming the "New Law." It is interesting to note that this is not the first time such an attempt has been made to subvert the law and the lives of so many, many people and will probably not be the last. That is why those in the know from all religions and political ideologies are getting extremely concerned and very nervous.

CHAPTER SEVEN
SHADOW PEOPLE FOR A SHADOW WORLD

So that is the core of this work, that there is a group of mysterious men and women working in the shadows to reform the human race and this planet in accordance with some long running plan. The attempts to weed out those considered to be defectives and create a basically homogenous human race in the image of what we might refer to as the Aryan race makes it appear that those who created us may be planning on a comeback. Certainly it is clear that they have a number of agents working among us. But there is certainly more to it than that. Let's look deeper.

Much of the activity that seems to begin with those who prefer to hide in the shadows deals with the control of the human race, right down to what individual humans look like. The "perfect" member of this perfect race is referred to as Aryan, a term which has a somewhat vague definition. For example, the word is actually Indo-Iranian though it is no longer in technical use. In Nazism and neo-Nazism, a non-Jewish Caucasian, especially one of Nordic type, supposed to be part of a master race.

It is one of the ironies of history that the word Aryan, which nowadays referring to the blond-haired, blue-eyed physical ideal of Nazi Germany, originally referred to a people who looked vastly different from the modern stereotype. Its history starts with the ancient Indo-Iranians, Indo-European peoples who inhabited parts of what are now Iran, Afghanistan, and India. Their tribal self-designation was a word reconstructed as *arya- or *ārya-. The first of these is the form found in the Iranian language, as ultimately in the name of *Iran* itself (from Middle Persian *Ērān (šahr),* "(Land) of the Iranians," from the genitive plural of *Ēr,* "Iranian"). The variant *ārya- is found unchanged in Sanskrit, where it referred to the upper crust of ancient Indian society. These words became known to European scholars in the 18th century.

The shifting of meaning that eventually led to the present-day sense that the Aryans were a tall blonde people started in the 1830s, when Friedrich Schlegel, a German scholar who was an important early Indo-Europeanist, came up with a theory that linked the Indo-Iranian words with the German word *Ehre,* "honor," and older Germanic names containing the element ario-, such as the Swiss warrior Ariovistus who was written about by Julius Caesar. Schlegel theorized that far from being just a designation of the Indo-Iranians, the word *arya- had in fact been what the Indo-Europeans called themselves, meaning something like "the honorable people[60]." Thus "Aryan" came to be synonymous with "Indo-European," in the mind of many and in this sense entered the general scholarly consciousness of the day. Not much later, it was proposed that the original homeland of the Indo-Europeans had been in northern Europe.

Based upon this theory, it was but a small leap for many to think of the Aryans as having had come from northern European. While these theories were gaining in popularity, certain anti-Semitic scholars in Germany took to viewing the Jews in Germany as the main non-Aryan people because of their Semitic roots; a distinction thus arose in their minds between Jews and the "true Aryan" Germans, a distinction that later furnished unfortunate fodder for the racial theories of the Nazis.

The belief of many who deal in the esoteric world was that at the beginnings of history was an advanced race who rose to greats heights before being destroyed by lesser races. To many of the real believers, this advanced race that had so many secrets was the Aryan race. This was believed by many to be an age of heroes, great empires, and gods walking the face of the world as well as unbelievable wealth available to a select few.

---

[60]This theory has since been called into question

The secrets of this ancient race are said to be passed down through such secret societies such as Freemasonry said to one of the oldest of these organizations still in existence today. Papyrus scrolls that were found by archeologists in 1888 in excavations in the Libyan desert describe secret meetings of similar groups as far back as 2000 B.C. These brotherhoods had already been involved in the building of the Temple of Solomon and fulfilled then their functions similar to today's unions, yet they already had a mystical tradition.

Figure 25: Masonic Symbol

The objective of Masonry is given as the inner transformation through spiritual perfection in reverence of God. Since Freemasons belong to all different religions, they call this God the "Great Builder of All Worlds".

Further references to such ancient traditions have been found in the Egyptian Book of the Dead and the God Thoth who had been their Grand Master. "Grand Master" is the usual title for the highest leaders of such secret orders. The spiritual knowledge of the Freemasons had been replaced by symbols, allegories and rituals which served communication. A secret language was created with symbols, for example, the Masonic ritual handshake, the pyramid, the pentagram, the use of the numbers 3, 7, 13 and 33 in coats of arms, emblems and today in company logos and names.

It should be kept in mind that the most important symbol in many secret organizations, including Freemasonry, is the apron. The apron, which at the outset was simple and unadorned, was replaced by the priesthood of Melchizedek around 2200 B.C. by a white lambskin and is still used like that today. In ancient Egypt, the Gods, who according to old traditions were flying the "Divine Ships", were represented in temple paintings wearing the apron.

Later, the priests wore the apron as a sign of devotion to the "flying Gods" and as a sign of authority, that they were representing the Gods who ruled over the people. The members of the "Brotherhood of the

Snake" already wore the apron as early as 3400 B.C. to show their submission to the Gods who came from heaven in what were described as "flying wheels". Though it is in wide spread use, it is doubtful that the lower grades of the different lodges today know the initial use of the apron.

BROTHERHOOD OF THE SNAKE

In addition to the Freemasons who claim to have a very early founding date, there was another ancient organization that may well pre-date it according to the Sumerian records. It was named after one of the animals of power in Sumerian belief. Of all of the animals revered in ancient human societies, none were as prominent or as important as the snake. As a result of this popularity, the snake was the logo of a group which had become very influential in early human societies of both Hemispheres. That group was a disciplined Brotherhood dedicated to the dissemination of spiritual knowledge and the attainment of spiritual freedom for the human race. This Brotherhood of the Snake[61] (also known as the "Brotherhood of the Serpent,") opposed the enslavement of spiritual beings and, according to ancient Egyptian

Figure 26: Brotherhood of the Snake Symbol

---

[61]Perhaps we are actually referring to what has become known as Reptilians.

writings, it sought to liberate the human race from what was referred to as Custodial bondage[62].

Legend says that it was the Brotherhood also imparted scientific knowledge and encouraged the high aesthetics that existed in many of the ancient secret societies. For these and other reasons, the snake had become a venerated symbol to humans and, according to Egyptian and biblical texts, an object of Custodial hatred.

Though this organization was founded eons ago, there are numerous references in Sumerian records regarding the history and interworkings of the Brotherhood. When we look to discover who founded the Brotherhood, Mesopotamian texts point right back to that rebellious "God," Prince Ea[63]. According to the research of Zacharia Sitchin, Ea was the oldest son of the King and the commander of the mission sent to earth from the planet Nibiru. Ancient Mesopotamian tablets relate that Ea and his father, Anu, possessed profound ethical and spiritual knowledge. This was the same knowledge that was later symbolized as trees in the Biblical Adam and Eve story.

From the research reported in Sitchin's ground breaking series, "The Earth Chronicles", the Biblical tree symbol came from pre-Biblical Mesopotamian works, such as one showing a snake wrapped around the trunk of a tree, identical to later portrayals of the snake in Eden. From the tree in the Mesopotamian depiction hang two pieces of fruit. To the right of the tree is the half-moon symbol of Ea; to the left is the planet symbol of Anu. The drawing indicates that Ea and Anu were associated with the snake and its teachings. This connection is affirmed by other Mesopotamian texts which describe Anu's palace in the "heavens" as being guarded by a God of the Tree of Truth and a God of the Tree of Life.

In one instance, Ea reportedly sent a human from earth to Nibiru be educated in that very knowledge:

---

[62] Because Brotherhood teachings included physical healing through spiritual means, the snake also came to symbolize physical healing. Today the snake is featured on the logo of the American Medical Association.

[63] For more information on this individual I would refer you to Zacharia Sitchin's work.

> Adapa [the name of an early man], thou art going before Anu, the King;
> The road to Heaven thou wilt take.
> When to Heaven thou has ascended, and hast approached the gate of Anu, the "Bearer of Life" and the "Grower of Truth" at the gate of Anu will be standing.

We therefore find Ea designated as the reputed culprit who tried to teach early man the way to personal knowledge and spiritual freedom. This suggests that while originally Ea intended his creation, Homo Sapien, to be suited primarily for Earth labor, at some point he changed his mind about using mental or spiritual enslavement as a means to control the newly developing race. He seems to have felt that free will had a place in the scheme of the world. There does not appear any doubt that Ea was what we might call goodhearted. Ea spoke before the councils of the gods on behalf of the new Earth race. He was against the cruelties the other gods were imposing on the humans that served them. Ea's wishes were always overruled by the other faction. Ea did not intend for the human race to be treated harshly.

Clearly, if Ea was a true historical personality as the Sumerians claimed, then he was the probable leader of the Brotherhood at its founding on Earth. The Brotherhood may have adopted the snake as its logo because Ea's first home on Earth was said to have been constructed in a serpent-infested swampland which Ea called Snake Marsh. Another possible explanation for the snake logo is offered by Zacharia Sitchin who says that the biblical word for "snake" is nahash, which comes from the root word NHSH, meaning "to decipher, to find out."

Despite all of their reported good intentions, the legendary Ea and early Brotherhood clearly failed in their goal to free the human race from domination by the Annunaki. Ancient Mesopotamian, Egyptian, and biblical texts relate that the "snake" was quickly defeated by other Custodial factions. The Bible informs us that the serpent in the Garden of Eden was overcome before it was able to complete its mission and give

Adam and Eve the "fruit" from the second "tree." Ea[64] (who was also symbolized as a snake) was banished to Earth and was extensively villainized by his opponents to ensure that he could never again secure a widespread following among human beings.

Ea's title was changed from "Prince of Earth" to "Prince of Darkness." He was labeled other horrible epithets: Satan, the Devil, Evil Incarnate, Monarch of Hell, Lord of Vermin, Prince of Liars, and more. He was portrayed as the mortal enemy of a Supreme Being and as the keeper of Hell. In fact, he was designated as all that was and is evil. People were taught that his only intentions were to spiritually enslave everyone and that everything bad on Earth was caused by him. Religious leaders routinely encouraged their followers to detect him in all of his future lives ("incarnations") and to destroy him and his creations whenever he was discovered.

Figure 27: Baphomet/Satan

All beliefs and practices named after his various appellations ("Satanism," "Devil Worship," etc.) were to be made so horrific and degrading that no right-thinking person would (or should) have anything to do with them. He and his followers came to be viewed by human beings with nothing but the utmost loathing.

This is not to say that Ea was actually portrayed by ancient Sumerians as some sort of saint. Clearly he was not, he was frankly just a man with all of man's flaws. He was actually described in ancient Mesopotamian texts as a being with certain distinct character flaws. If Ea was in fact a real person, then he appears to have, on one hand, been a genius who could get things done, but who was often careless about

---

[64] Perhaps the original entity that was symbolized as Satan or the fallen Angel referred to in the Bible.

anticipating the consequences of how he went about accomplishing his goals. By genetically engineering a work race (what we call Homo sapiens), Ea wound up giving his enemies a powerful tool of spiritual repression. Ea then appears to have compounded the blunder by founding and/or empowering the early Snake Brotherhood. It was a tremendous effort and came very close to succeeding, but alas, it was overpowered by the sheer might of the Annunaki and, after its reported defeat, the Brotherhood was taken over and continued to remain a powerful force in human affairs, but under the domination of the very Custodial factions that Ea and the original Brotherhood were said to have opposed.

History indicates that the Brotherhood was turned under its new Custodial "Gods" into a chilling weapon of spiritual repression and betrayal, despite the efforts of many sincere humanitarians to bring about true spiritual reform through Brotherhood channels all the way up until today. By reportedly creating a work race and the Brotherhood of the Snake, the "God" Ea had helped build a trap for billions of spiritual beings on Earth.

As we shall now begin to carefully document, the Brotherhood of the Snake has been the world's most effective tool for preserving mankind's status as a spiritually ignorant creature of toil throughout all of history. Evidence supports the position that during all of that time, and continuing today, the Brotherhood and its network of organizations have remained intimately tied to the UFO phenomenon. This corruption of the Brotherhood, and the overwhelming effect it would have on human society, was already apparent by the year 2000 B.C. in ancient Egypt— the next stop on our journey.

Thus, as we can see there were, and apparently still are actually two camps, the "gods" who would keep man in ignorance and the group, name unknown, that would share knowledge with man. There are certainly a number of correlations between various groups today and the two groups that struggled over the fate of man eons ago.

CHAPTER EIGHT
ANCIENT ORDERS

The rule of the Annunaki over the human race was direct for eons, but then something happened. Something so massive that it caused the Annunaki to pull away from their seats of unlimited power on earth. They were forced to rule from afar, through the actions of others.

According to no less a source than the Holy Bible, having interbred with the daughters of man, the "gods" had given birth to a race of hybrids, known as great men of old, who were now thrust into the seats of power. These demi-gods, as they were called, were the spokesmen for the gods. They held their power as a result of the will of the gods. This appointment by the Annunaki of their children to rule mankind became known as the divine right of these demi-gods to rule.

Figure 28: James VI of Scotland

DIVINE RIGHT OF KINGS

When the Stewart King James VI of Scotland ascended the throne of England to become King James I of Great Britain, he made a speech that shocked and appalled the nobles sitting in Parliament. They had been becoming increasingly bold over the previous few years, attempting to limit the powers of the crown in order to strengthen their own. What shocked them was that James used his coronation speech to remind them of the ancient, traditional belief that a monarch is chosen by God to be His emissary and representative on Earth, and ought therefore to be responsible to no one but God. In other words, James was asserting what has become known to history as 'The Divine Right of Kings', and they didn't like it one bit.

Quotes from the James's coronation speech show how inflammatory James' words actually were at the time:

"The state of monarchy is the most supreme thing upon earth, for kings are not only God's lieutenants upon earth, and sit upon God's throne, but even by God himself are called gods... In the Scriptures, kings are called gods, and so their power after a certain relation compared to divine power. Kings are also compared to fathers of families: for a king is truly Parens Patriae, the politique father of his people... Kings are justly called gods, for that they exercise a manner of resemblance of divine power upon earth: for if you will consider the attributes to God, you shall see how they agree in the person of a king."

The nobles were aghast at what they just heard. This fat, bloated wastrel was telling everyone to worship him as a god! It seemed patently ridiculous to everyone listening. Even more offensive to everyone in the room, James finished up his speech by putting Parliament in its place basically telling them that, since he ruled by the grace of God, any act or word spoken in contradiction of him was an act against God himself. James continued:

"I conclude then this point, touching the power of kings with this axiom of divinity: that as to dispute what God may do is blasphemy... so is it sedition in subjects to dispute what a king may do in the height of his power. I would not have you meddle with such ancient rights of mine as I have received from my predecessors... All novelties are dangerous as well in a politic as in a natural body, and therefore I would loathe to be

quarreled in my ancient rights and possessions, for that were to judge me unworthy of that which my predecessors had and left me."

James had just re-established the divine right of kings to rule with absolute power. Although it was James I that made the concept famous, he certainly did not invent the idea of rule Divine Right. The concept that a King is subject to no earthly authority is as old as civilization itself. But the question is where James came up with the idea, as nothing in his past would suggest that he felt this way.

Perhaps a look at his history would give the reader some idea of where he acquired such strange ideas. James VI of Scotland was the only child of Mary, Queen of Scots. James' father was Lord Darnley (Henry Stewart) who had been killed in a suspicious explosion. There was a rumor that began shortly after his death that the explosion was caused by Mary and Lord Bothwell, the man whom she would later marry.

When James was thirteen months of age, Mary was forced to abdicate in his favor. James became the King of Scotland and never saw his mother again, although at one point before her execution he did make some contact with her during an ill-hatched plot to restore her to the throne. While Mary was in prison in London she tried to send presents to James, but Elizabeth I would not let them be sent to Scotland.

James had been baptized as a Catholic because of his mother's faith but was brought up under the influence of a reformed Protestant Scotland. He was educated by a variety of tutors and was known for his great knowledge. James later wrote and published many poems and translated French works. He wrote many books during his lifetime on such various topics as tobacco, kingship and witchcraft. He instigated several religious changes declaring Christmas, Good Friday, Easter, Ascension and Whit Sunday as Holy Days. Among the earth shaking changes, were that the Holy Communion could be given privately to the aged and sick and communion should be taken kneeling. Children at eight years old were to be confirmed and Baptism could take place at home, if necessary. These five changes were the Five Articles of Perth.

The Church of Scotland would not accept these changes but through means of bribery and blackmail, James forced through the changes. He ordered the translation of ancient Greek and Hebrew into English as the King James Version of the Bible. Having been raised with a strong religious belief, James loathed violence and was very insecure.

He was somewhat paranoid and thus easily led. In fact, he wore heavily padded clothing most of his life as a method of protecting himself from being stabbed. The last Regent for James was the Earl of Morton who had been a ringleader in the killing of Darnley and Rissio (Mary Queen of Scot's trusted counselor and confidant). Morton is reported to have been a "crude, uneducated thug" but his strength kept Scotland together. He kept in favor with Elizabeth, defeated the Catholics who were trying to restore Mary and kept the Protestant ministers from taking over the government.

The Earls of Argyll and Atholl opposed Morton. Morton's plan was to resign the regency and control the government from behind the scenes. During this struggle for power, the young Earl of Mar who was a Morton supporter stormed into Stirling Castle and captured the King. James was terrified. Mar had been his old guardian's son and a playmate as a child. He learned that you could trust no one.

After the raid at Stirling, he found a friend and protector, Esme Stuart, whom he made Duke of Lennox. Esme had spent most of his life in France and was educated and sophisticated. There is a great deal of evidence that Esme was also deeply involved in esoteric groups, which were numerous on the continent. Morton had given James a certain amount of power and as his self-confidence grew, Morton found that he could no longer control the young King. When Morton was accused by James Stewart of being in on the plot to kill Darnley, James did nothing to protect Morton who was eventually executed.

It is believed that the relationship between Lennox and James was a homosexual one. Records show that it was the Duke of Lennox who put forth the idea to James of the divine right of Kings, that he was above the people and the Church, whereas Knox and the Presbyterians thought that the King should rule Scotland for God and be an ordinary member of the Kirk.

In "Trew Law of Free Monarchies" James wrote:

"Out of the law of God, the duty, and allegiance of the people to their lawful King, their obedience, I say, ought to be to him, as to God's Lieutenant in earth, obeying his commands in all things, except directly against God, as the commands of Gods Minister, acknowledging him a Judge set by God over them, having power to judge them, but to be judged only by God."

James used his power to appoint bishops as a way of controlling the Church. Lennox encouraged the King to hunt and hold wild parties instead of governing the country. The English ambassador, Robert Bowes, said "*Lennox's greatness is greatly increased, and the King so much affected to him that he delights only in his company, and thereby Lennox carries the sway.*"

Needless to say, Lennox was very unpopular with the Kirk. James was kidnapped by the Earl of Gowrie at Ruthven Castle where he had spent the night after hunting. James took this to heart and apparently decided that it was time to stop the exotic living. Also, After Mary was executed, James had to keep one crucial consideration in mind and that was the succession to the throne of England. He became adept at playing a balancing game, playing off one Scottish faction against the other while keeping on friendly terms with Elizabeth.

As harsh and dictatorial as it may seem, such a system actually protected the rights of individual citizens from even larger and more powerful bullies such as the Parliament and the Pope. When power rests ultimately in the hands of a single individual such as a king, beholden to nobody except God, who need not appease anyone for either money or votes, injustices are more likely to be righted after a direct appeal to him. Furthermore, past monarchs who held their claims to power doggedly in the face of increasing opposition from the Catholic Church managed, as long as they held their power, to save their subjects from the forced religious indoctrination and social servitude that comes with a Catholic theocracy.

In fact, Stephen Coston[65] wrote that:

"Without the doctrine of the Divine Right, Roman Catholicism would have dominated history well beyond its current employment in the Dark Ages. Furthermore, Divine Right made it possible for the Protestant Reformation in England to take place, mature and spread to the rest of the world."

The Divine Right of Kings practiced by European monarchs was actually based on a more ancient doctrine practiced by the monarchs of Judah and Israel in the Old Testament. Many European royal families considered them to be their ancestors, tracing their royal European lineage back to the Jewish King David, sometimes through the descendants of Jesus Christ. Such a line of descent was (and is) known as the "Grail Bloodline[66]."

GRAIL BLOODLINE

There were many stories in Europe of the various royal families being descended form Christ. Supposedly the Merovingian Bloodline was founded by a child of Christ and through intermarriage with other royal families his blood spread through the various royal Houses of Europe.

One of Europe's most famous monarchs, Charlemagne the Great, King of France was often called "David" in reference to his famous ancestor, and the Habsburg King Otto was called "the son of David." In fact, the European tradition of anointing kings comes from that practiced

---

[65]Coston, Stephen, Sources of English Constitutional History, 1972
[66] Baigent, Michael, Richard Leigh, and Henry Lincoln, "Holy Blood, Holy Grail,", Delacorte Press (October 25, 2005)

in the Old Testament. George Athas[67] describes how the ceremony symbolized the Lord Yahweh adopting the new king as his own son:

"Firstly, the king was the 'Anointed' of Yahweh - the mesiach, from which we derive the term 'Messiah.' At his anointing (or his coronation), the Spirit of Yahweh entered the king, giving him superhuman qualities and allowing him to carry out the dictates of the deity. The psalmist of Psalm 45 describes the king as 'fairer than the sons of men', and continued to praise his majestic characteristics. This king also had eternal life granted to him by Yahweh. The deity is portrayed as saying to him, 'You are my son - today I have sired you.' The king was Yahweh's Firstborn - the bekhor - who was the heir to his father's estate. He was 'the highest of the kings of the earth.' Thus, the king was adopted by Yahweh at his coronation and, as such, was in closer communion with the deity than the rest of the people. On many occasions, Yahweh was called the king's god.

The king was distinguished far above the ordinary mortal, rendering him holy and his person sacred. It was regarded as a grievous offence to lay a hand on him. Thus, to overthrow the king was rebellion of the most heinous sort and an affront to the deity who had appointed the king... We can note that the King of Judah and Israel is described in divine terms. He is, for example, seen as sitting at Yahweh's right hand, and his adopted son. We find similar motifs of Pharaohs seated to the right of a deity of Egypt. Psalm 45:7 calls the king an 'elohim' - a god. Psalm 45:7also says 'Your throne is like God's throne.'"

Here we see the basis for King James' claim that the scriptures likened human kings to gods. As such, kings were strongly associated with the priesthood as well, and in some cases took on priestly functions. Traditionally, the Jewish priesthood was dominated by the Cohens of the Tribe of Levi, which was biologically related but functionally separate

---

[67] Athas, George, The Tel Dan Inscription: A Reappraisal And a New Interpretation (Journal for the Study of the Old Testament Supplement), T. & T. Clark Publishers (January 30, 2006)

from the royal line of David - that is, until Jesus came along, heir to both the kingly and priestly titles through his lineage back to both tribes.

However, in other more ancient cultures, such as the Egyptians, the royal and priestly functions were inseparable. In addition to regarding their Pharaohs as the literal offspring of deities, and in fact, deities themselves, the Egyptians believed that the gods had given them the institution of kingship itself. Their first king had been one of their main gods: Osiris, whom all human kings were expected to emulate. Richard Cassaro, in his book, A Deeper Truth, elaborates:

"... during the First Time [The Golden Age when the gods ruled directly on Earth] a human yet eternal king named Osiris initiated a monarchial government in Egypt and imparted a wise law and spiritual wisdom to the people. At the end of his ministry, Osiris left his throne to the people. It was, thereafter, the duty of every king to rule over Egypt in the same manner Osiris had ruled."

This concept that kingship began with a single divine ruler of whom all subsequent human kings are descendants can be traced back to the oldest civilization acknowledged by history, Sumeria, and the other Mesopotamian cultures that followed, such as the Assyrians and the Babylonians. To quote Henri Frankfort[68]:

"In Mesopotamia, the king was regarded as taking on godhood at his coronation, and at every subsequent New Year festival. However, he was often seen as having been predestined to the divine throne by the gods at his birth, or even at the beginning of time. Through a sacred marriage, he had a metaphysical union with the mother goddess, who filled him with life, fertility, and blessing, which he passed onto his people."

---

[68]Frankfort, Henri, Kingship and the Gods: A Study of Ancient Near Eastern Religion as the Integration of Society and Nature (Oriental Institute Essays), Oriental Institute Of The University Of (July 15, 1978)

There were actually three types of divine or sacred kingship that were recognized by the people of the ancient world. The king was seen as a receptacle of supernatural or divine power, given him directly by the gods. Secondly, the king was seen as a divine or semi-divine ruler and finally, the individual who was anointed as king was seen as the agent or mediator of the sacred power of the gods.

However, when all is said and done, it is probably closest to the truth to say that all of these concepts stem from the almost universal belief that kingship descended from Heaven with a single divine being who was literally thought of as the ancestor of all those who followed. This king, was known to the ancients as Kronos, the Forgotten Father, and this is another name for the deity/planet, Saturn. He was the 'brightest star in the heavens", who fell to Earth and intermarried with the wives of men to breed a race of human kings (the Grail Bloodline). After that he was imprisoned in the Underworld by his father, Zeus, the Most High God, for disobeying a social taboo against interbreeding with humans, and sharing secret knowledge with them.

Some might think this contradicts the traditional association of ancient kings with the Sun-God, but in fact, Saturn himself was a sun god of a sort. In ancient times Saturn was the dominant figure in the night sky and as such became known as 'the midnight sun' (a term later used by occultists to refer to the Grail). From its position in the sky it appeared to stand still, as the rest of the night sky revolved around it. It was therefore also called 'The Central Sun.'

David Talbott[69] has an interesting view regarding the origin of kingship. From a piece he wrote entitled "*Saturn as a Stationary Sun and Universal Monarch*', he stated:

"*A global tradition recalls an exemplary king ruling in the sky before kings ever ruled on earth.*"

---

[69] Talbott, David, The Saturn Myth: A Reinterpretation of Rites and Symbols Illuminating Some of the Dark Corners of Primordial Society, Doubleday & Company; (1980).

This mythical figure appears as the first in the line of kings, the father of kings, the model of the good king. But this same figure is commonly remembered by early man as the central luminary of the sky, often as a central sun, an unmoving sun, or superior sun ruling before the present sun.

And most curiously, with the rise of the science of astronomy this celestial 'king' was identified as the planet Saturn."

One can see traces of this ancient progenitor of kings just in the word 'monarchy' itself. The syllable "mon" means "one" in Indo-European language systems, as in "The One King Who Rules Over All." But in Egypt, "Mon" was one of the names of the sun god, (also called Amun-Re) in its occluded state, at night, when the sun, as they saw it, passed beneath the Earth. The word meant literally for them, "The Hidden One", because he ruled the world (and the Underworld) from his secret subterranean prison.

The syllable "ark" comes from the Greek "arche", meaning "original", or "originator." As the first "monarch", Kronos was the originator of kings, the Forgotten Father of all royal bloodlines. Many of our commonly associated symbols of kingship date back to the time when Kronos first introduced it, and are directly derived from him.

For instance, the crown symbolizes the (central) sun, the "Godhead" descending upon the brow of the wise king. The Sumerian kings adorned their crowns with horns, just like Kronos was believed to have done. The throne was Kronos' seat on his celestial boat in heaven, and has also been passed down to us. Kronos and his descendants were known as Shepherd Kings, an appellation used by royalty throughout history, and this is the origin of the king's scepter, which was once a shepherd's staff. The coronation stone and the orb surmounted by a cross are also Saturnian/solar symbols, and the Egyptian word for the sun, Re, may be the source of the French word for king, Roi.

Kronos, and the god-kings who followed him, were known by the title "Lord of the Four Corners of the World." This has given birth to the universal, recurring archetype of "Le Roi du Monde", a concept that was brilliantly explored in a book by René Guenon[70] of the same name. In a surprising number of cultures throughout the world and throughout history, there exists this concept of "The Lord of the Earth", an omnipresent and eternal monarch who reigns from within the very center of the Earth itself, directing events on the surface with his superhuman psyche. In the Judeo-Christian tradition, "The Lord of the Earth" is a term applied to Satan, or Lucifer, who, like Saturn, was the brightest star in Heaven, but was cast down by God. Like Saturn, he was imprisoned inside the bowels of the Earth, in a realm called Hell.

In fact, it is quite clear that the figure of Satan comes from Saturn, the "Fish-Goat-Man", and obviously the two words are etymologically related. Perhaps this is why the "Grail Bloodline", the divine lineage from which all European kings have come, is traced by many back to Lucifer. The medieval Christian heretics, based in the Languedoc region of southern France known as the Cathars took this concept to its logical conclusion. They insisted that, since Satan is the 'King of the World' ("Rex Mundi', as they called him), and Jehovah was, in the Bible, the one who created the world, Jehovah and Satan must be one and the same. For preaching this they were massacred unto extinction by the Papacy under the guise of a Crusade that was organized to stamp out heretics in Europe.

However, in the Eastern tradition, "the Lord of the Earth" represents the ultimate incarnate manifestation of Godhood. They too see him as ruling his kingdom from the center of the Earth, in a subterranean city called either Shamballah or Agartha. And in this tradition, the Lord of the Earth is also a super-spiritual being capable of incarnating on the surface of the Earth in a series of 'Avatars', or human kings who rule various eras of existence.

According to author Alice Bailey[71]:

"Shamballa is the seat of the 'Lord of the World', who has made the sacrifice (analogous to the Bodhisattva's vow) of remaining to watch

---

[70] Guenon, Rene, The King of the World, Sophia Perennis (June 25, 2004).
[71] Bailey, Alice, A Treatise on White Magic or The Way of the Disciple, Lucis Publishing Company (June 1998).

over the evolution of men and devas until all have been 'saved' or enlightened."

One of the names that the Hindus use for "The Lord of the Earth" is Manu, who, writes Guenon[72], is,

"a cosmic intelligence that reflects pure spiritual light and formulates the law (Dharma) appropriate to the conditions of our world and our cycle of existence."

Ferdinand Ossendowski[73] added:

"The Lord of the World is in touch with the thoughts of all those who direct the destiny of mankind... He knows their intentions and their ideas. If they are pleasing to God, the Lord of the World favors them with his invisible aid. But if they are displeasing to God, he puts a check on their activities."

These are obviously activities that human kings, as incarnations of the Lord of the Earth, are expected to replicate in their own kingdoms to the best of their ability. In fact, a number of human kings throughout history have been viewed by their subjects as incarnations of the "Lord of the Earth", embodying the concepts that he represents. These include Charlemagne, Alexander the Great (who was believed to have horns literally growing from his head, just like Saturn), and Melchizedek, a mysterious priest-king mentioned repeatedly in the Old Testament and imbued with an inexplicable importance. He was called the "Prince of Salem" (as in Jeru-Salem), and is said to have shared bread and wine with Abraham on Mt. Moriah. Some believe that the cup which they used is the artifact that later became known as the Holy Grail.

---

[72] Guenon, Rene, The King of the World, Sophia Perennis (June 25, 2004).
[73] Ossendowski, Ferdinand, Beasts, Men And Gods, NuVision Publications, LLC (December 1, 2006)

Some have also identified him with another king of Jerusalem, Adonizedek, and with Shem, Noah's son. Nobody knows what his ancestry is, who his descendants might have been, or why, thousands of years later, Jesus Christ was referred to in the scriptures as, "A priest according to the Order of Melchizedek."

Of Melchizedek's significance, René Guenon[74] writes:

"Melchizedek, or more precisely, Melki-Tsedeq, is none other than the title used by Judeo-Christian tradition to denote the function of 'The Lord of the World'...

Melki-Tsedeq is thus both king and priest. His name means 'King of Justice', and he is also king of Salem, that is, of 'Peace', so again we find 'Justice' and "Peace', the fundamental attributes pertaining to the 'Lord of the World.'"

Even more pertinent information is provided by researcher Julius Evola[75], who in his book The Mystery of the Grail wrote:

"In some Syrian texts, mention is made of a stone that is the foundation or center of the world, hidden in the 'primordial depths, near God's temple. It is put in relation with the body of the primordial man (Adam) and, interestingly enough, with an inaccessible mountain place, the access to which must not be revealed to other people; here Melchizedek, 'in divine and eternal service', watches over Adam's body. In Melchizedek we find again the representation of the supreme function of the Universal Ruler, which is simultaneously regal and priestly; here this representation is associated with some kind of guardian of Adam's body who originally possessed the Grail and who, after losing it, no longer lives. This is found together with the motifs of a mysterious stone and an inaccessible seat."

---

[74] Guenon, Rene, The King of the World, Sophia Perennis (June 25, 2004).
[75] Evola, Julius, The Mystery of the Grail: Initiation and Magic in the Quest for the Spirit, Inner Traditions (November 1, 1996).

Clearly, that foundation stone of the world is the same as the Black, or Hidden Sun in the center of the Earth, or the 'Grail Stone' which is said to be hidden in that location. The Grail Romances provide us with much insight into the 'King of the World' concept. He is represented in the story by one of the supporting characters, Prester John, a king who is mentioned in passing as ruling over a spiritual domain in the faraway East, and who, quite fittingly, is said to come from Davidic descent.

Evola continued:

"The Tractatus pulcherrimus referred to him as 'king of kings' rex regnum. He combined spiritual authority with regal power... Yet essentially, 'Prester John' is only a title and a name, which designates not a given individual but rather a function. Thus in Wolfram von Eschenbach and in the Titurel we find 'Prester John' as a title; the Grail, as we will see, indicates from time to time the person who must become Prester John. Moreover, in the legend, 'Prester John' designates one who keeps in check the people of Gog and Magog, who exercises a visible and invisible dominion, figuratively, dominion over both natural and invisible beings, and who defends the access of his kingdom with 'lions' and 'giants.' In this kingdom is also found the 'fountain of youth.'"

"The dignity of a sacred king is often accompanied by biblical reminiscences, by presenting Prester John as the son or nephew of King David, and sometimes as King David himself... 'David, King of the Hindus, who is called by the people 'Prester John' - the King (Prester John) descends from the son of King David."

The "Lord of the Earth", or the figures that represent him, are often symbolized by a victory stone, or a foundation stone which is emblematic of their authority. For instance, British kings are crowned on the "Stone of Destiny", believed to have been used as a pillow by Jacob in the Old Testament. Such a stone is often referred to in mythology as having fallen from Heaven, like the Grail Stone, which fell out of Lucifer's crown during his war with God, and became the foundation stone for the Grail kingdom, having the power, as it is written, to 'make kings.' Because it fell from Heaven, the Grail is also often associated with a falling star, like that which Lucifer represents. Of course the Black Sun in the center of the Earth also represents Rex Mundi's victory stone. It is interesting, then, that in the Babylonian tongue, the word "tsar" means "rock", and is not only an anagram of "star", but a word that in the Russian language refers to an imperial monarch.

Sometimes the monarchial foundation stone is represented as a mountain, especially the World or Primordial Mountain that in mythology provides the Earth with its central axis. The Sumerians referred to this as Mt. Mashu. Its twin peaks were said to reach up to Heaven, while the tunnels and caves within it reached down to the depths of Hell. Jehovah in the Bible, sometimes called El Shaddai ("The Lord of the Mountain") had Mt. Zion for a foundation stone, and was believed to actually live inside of the mountain. Later, the kingdom of Jesus Christ was said to be "founded upon the Rock of Sion".

The stone that fell from Heaven, the royal victory stone, is also sometimes depicted under the symbolic form of a castrated phallus, such as that of Kronos, whose disembodied penis was hurled into the ocean, and there spawned the Lady Venus. This story is a recapitulation of the Osiris story, as well as the inspiration for the Grail legends, in which the Fisher King is wounded in the genitals, causing the entire kingdom to fall under a spell of perpetual malaise. The only thing that can heal the king, and therefore the kingdom is the Grail. This is a recurring theme in world mythology. The king and/or the kingdom that temporarily falls asleep or falls under a magic spell which renders it/him ineffectual for a time, until the stars are right, or the proper conditions are met. This causes the king and his kingdom to reawaken, to rise from the ashes, from the tomb, or often, to rise out of the sea.

The cycle recurs in the tales of the Lord of the Earth, who alternates between periods of death-like sleep within his tomb in the center of the Earth, and rebirth, in which he once again returns to watch over his kingdom, to restore righteousness and justice to the land. He then presides over a new, revitalized "Golden Age".

Julius Evola writes of the archetype:

"It is a theme that dates back to the most ancient times and that bears a certain relation to the doctrine of the 'cyclical manifestations' or avatars, namely, the manifestation, occurring at special times and in various forms, of a single principle, which during intermediate periods exists in an unmanifested state. Thus every time a king displayed the traits of an incarnation of such a principle, the idea arose in the legend that he has not died but has withdrawn into an inaccessible seat whence once day he will manifest, or that he is asleep and will awaken one day... The image of a regality in a state of sleep or apparent death, however, is akin to that of an altered, wounded, paralyzed regality, in regard not to its intangible principle but to its external and historical representatives.

Hence the theme of the wounded, mutilated or weakened king who continues to live in an inaccessible center, in which time and death are suspended.... In the Hindu tradition we encounter the theme of Mahaksyapa, who sleeps in a mountain but will awaken at the sound of shells at the time of the new manifestation of the principle that previously manifested itself in the form of Buddha. Such a period is also that of the coming of a Universal Ruler (cakravartin) by the name of Samkha. Since samkha means 'shells', this verbal assimilation expresses the idea of the awakening from sleep of the new manifestation of the King of the World and of the same primordial tradition that the above-mentioned legend conceives to be enclosed (during the intermediate period of crisis) in a shell. When the right time comes, in conformity with the cyclical laws, a new manifestation from above will occur (Kalki-avatara) in the form of a sacred king who will triumph over the Dark Age.

"...many people thought that the Roman world, in its imperial and pagan phase, signified the beginning of a new Golden Age, the king of which, Kronos, was believed to be living in a state of slumber in the Hyperborean region. During Augustus' reign, the Sibylline prophecies announced the advent of a 'solar' king, a rex a coelo, or ex sole missus, to

which Horace seems to refer when he invokes the advent of Apollo, the Hyperborean god of the Golden Age. "

Rene Guenon believed in this concept, and that the periods of slumber for the Lord of the Earth have been cyclically brought to a close by apocalypses. After this, Le Roi du Monde would return to clean up the wreckage and once more look after his faithful flock. In the Revelation of St. John the Divine, three kings actually return from periods of slumber, death, or prolonged absence: Jesus, Satan, and Jehovah, and naturally, the governmental entity that God chooses for this utopian world is the one which has always been associated with holiness and righteousness: monarchy.

Monarchy was the first form of government observed by man, and it was, according to almost every culture, created by God himself. It is the primordial, archetypal form of government, the most natural, that which all other forms of government vainly try to mimic, while at the same time violating its most basic tenets. Monarchy was, for thousands of years, all that man knew. The idea of not having a monarch, a father figure to watch over them, to maintain the community's relationship with the divine, represented to them, not freedom, but chaos, uncertainty, and within a short time, death. The common people did not jealously vie for positions of power, nor did they desire to have any say in the decision of who would be king. In fact, most of them preferred that there be no decision to make at all: most monarchies functioned on the principle of primogeniture, passing the scepter and crown down from father to son, or in some cases, through the matrilineal line. The decision was up to nature or God, so therefore just and righteous in itself.

Furthermore, they knew they could count on their king or queen to watch over them as they would their own children, to be fair and honest, to protect them from invasion, to maintain the proper relationship between God and the kingdom. They desired to make their kingdom on Earth reflect the order and perfection that existed in God's kingdom in Heaven.

And for thousands of years before the modern era, when 90% of the population was not intellectually capable of participating in government or making electoral decisions, monarchy stood as a bulwark against the disintegration of the societal unit, providing a stability that otherwise could not be achieved. If monarchy had not been invented, human history could never have happened.

Richard Russell Cassaro[76], in The Deeper Truth, said it best:

"Since the obligation of every king... is to maintain law, order, morality, spirituality, and religion within his kingdom, then the very design of a monarchy itself was probably conceived by the superior intelligence called God so as to endow mankind with a sound system of government. In other words, the concept of kingship was designed for, and delivered to, the peoples of earth by God to teach mankind to live in a humanized social environment... Human history, with its past and present kingdoms and kings - Egypt, Assyria, Persia, Babylon, Sumer, Aztec, Inca, Jordan, Saudi Arabia, Great Britain, to name a few - stands as a testimony to the fact that the monarchial form of government has been the basis for almost every civilization."

If monarchy is the most perfect form of government, and if it has been responsible for providing us with at least 6000 years of human history, why now does it seem to be only an ancient pretension? Why is the concept of having a monarchy actually function in government considered to be a quaint but laughable thing of the past? Have we really moved beyond monarchy?

Hardly. If you were to graph the entire 6000 years of known human history and isolate the period in which civilized nations have been without monarchs, it would be merely a blip on the spectrum. In fact, of the civilized Western nations, few do not have a monarch reigning either de jure or de facto (although they continue to elect Presidents from royal European lineage.) Most nations that maintain representational government still have a monarch either recognized by the government, or

---

[76] Cassaro, Richard Russell, The Deeper Truth: Uncovering the Missing History of Egypt, Triptych Press (December 24, 2000).

by the people at large. Although essentially powerless, these monarchs maintain a symbolic link between a nation and its heritage, its most sacred, most ancient traditions.

They also constitute a government-in-waiting, should the thin veneer of illusory 'freedom' and 'equality' that maintains democracy break down. The modern system of Republican government is based not so much on the freedom of the individual, but on the free flow of money, on debt, usury, and inflation, on a monetary house of cards known as "Fractional Reserve Lending." It would only take a major and slightly prolonged collapse of the monetary system to eliminate this governmental system. At that point, civilized man will have essentially two choices: anarchy or monarchy, and if people have any sense at all they will choose the latter, rather than subjecting themselves to a chaotic succession of despots interspersed with periods of violence and rioting, and the poverty that comes with the lack of a stable state.

It would be the most natural thing in the world for the royal families of Earth, as well as the monarchial system which they have maintained, and which has maintained us for thousands of years, to just slide right into place. The kingdom of the gods, who once ruled during man's Golden Age, would awaken from their slumber and heed the call to duty, like Kronos, their Forgotten Father, and monarch of all, who soundly sleeps within his tomb in the primordial mountain, waiting for his chance to once again hold dominion over the Earth.

This mission is at the core of many of the secret societies.

CHAPTER NINE
AGENTS OF THE UNSEEN

So now would be a good time for the reader to consider what to think about the scenario that has been laid out in the previous chapters. Is it really so hard to believe that this world is being manipulated by a super-secret organization that operates form the shadows, controlling the very mechanisms that make our society function. Are we the dominate species on this planet as we have always believed or are we merely the unwitting servants of an incredibly old, incredibly powerful ancient order? Are we the masters of all that we survey or the servants?

As if this is not enough for the reader to digest, there is still more that will certainly be considered bizarre. It is the belief of many that this advanced race of masters also uses what we refer to as the paranormal to influence humans.

Now this author does not think that there is anyone who would not agree that religion is a very strong control mechanism. No matter what the religion or who the "god" there is always a long list of dos and don'ts. Religions have been responsible for more wars, death and destruction than almost any other cause. Religion has been responsible for the destruction of entire civilizations and the death or millions of innocent lives. If the "gods" created religions, then it makes sense that we are all taught that we much obey the wishes of the gods. However, what about those who are not religious, how are they controlled or at least influenced. Perhaps for those individuals there are the paranormal, the world of the unseen.

We are all well aware of the familiar world around us, but few seem aware that there is an entirely different world that is generally referred to as the world of the paranormal. Now, with the dozens of books and the many television shows about ghosts and goblins, there is no doubt that most are aware of certain aspects of this other world, but there is a vast world of the unseen that is still a mystery to most.

Actually, for as long as there have been tales of hauntings and ghostly phenomena, there have been sightings of strange entities that people have come to refer to as the 'Shadow People'. These Shadow People are defined by their featureless, shadow-like appearance and the feeling of foreboding that most experience when these mysterious creatures are present. These shadows are nearly always described by witnesses as having a manly shape, large and with a broad silhouette and perhaps the strangest thing about them, is that they are usually seen wearing a hat of some sort. In some instances there are red eyes that seem to pierce right through you.

This author is the host of the Ken Hudnall Show[77] a paranormal radio show heard on http://www.borderlandradio.com. Callers to the show have related numerous stories of encounters with Shadow People. No one is ever sure exactly what the Shadow People are, but there seem little doubt that they are not 'normal ghosts'? Most people will say that they are not like anything they have ever seen. In fact, these entities don't usually seem to have purpose to their visits and from the bad feelings they emit, it seems that they aren't benign by any means.

One important observation about shadow people, that isn't often seen with 'conventional ghosts' is that they seem to be very much aware of our presence. A lot of the time manifestations occur involving an entity that seems to be going about daily business, rarely do they notice or try and communicate with people. The Shadow People tend to be very aware of our presence and in fact seem like they wish to make us feel uncomfortable or frightened. They do not attempt to communication, they

---

[77] The Ken Hudnall Show is heard Monday through Friday from 6:00-9:00 PM Mountain Time on http://www.blogtalkradio.com/ken-hudnall.

merely allow themselves to be seen which may in and of itself be a method of communication.

The real question is whether or not these shadow creatures are evil? It is tempting to say that they are, especially given the bad vibes they seem to let off to anyone with whom they come in contact. However, there is not much documentation to say that a bad occurrence usually follows a Shadow Man visitation. If fact, most visitations usually result in the apparition fading away, or disappearing when noticed. They never seem to talk or approach the witness, instead they simply are seen standing menacingly in doorways and corners.

Some people say that Shadow People are aliens or time traveling beings. This is an interesting theory, as it suggests that not only do these entities exist, but they are frequently visitors in our lives. There is the question as to why they seem to want to hang around us so much? Are we being studied by these creatures? Could this be why there are so many reports of 'feelings of evil' coming from these creatures?

What makes the Shadow People phenomena interesting, in the world of the supernatural, is the consistency in the sightings. No matter whether it's an old person or a child, or someone at any age in between, what they see is always the same. People on opposite ends of the world report seeing these entities on a daily basis and their recollections are strikingly similar. Whatever these Shadow People are they are definitely a regular occurrence in a lot of people's lives.

The beginnings of a visitation are always the same. You were sitting comfortably on your sofa reading the latest issue of FATE in the dim light when movement across the room caught your attention. It seemed dark and shadowy, but there was nothing there. You returned to your reading - and a moment later there it was again. You looked up quickly this time and saw the fleeting but distinctly human shape of the shadow pass quickly over the far wall... and disappear.

What was that? Some natural shadow? Your heightened imagination? A ghost? Or was it something that seems to be a spreading phenomenon - apparitions that are coming to be known as "shadow people" or "shadow beings." Perhaps this is an old phenomenon with a new name that is now being discussed more openly, in part thanks to the Internet. Or maybe it's a phenomenon that, for some reason, is manifesting with greater frequency and intensity now.

Those who are experiencing and studying the shadow people phenomenon say that these entities almost always used to be seen out of the corner of the eye and very briefly. But more and more, people are beginning to see them straight on and for longer periods of time. Some experiencers testify that they have even seen eyes, usually red, on these shadow beings.

The mysterious sightings have become a hot topic of conversion in paranormal chat rooms, message boards and websites, and it is given widespread attention on paranormal talk radio.

What are shadow people and where do they come from? Several theories have been offered.

THE IMAGINATION

The explanation we get from skeptics and mainstream science - and who are usually people who have never experienced the shadow people phenomenon - is that it is nothing more than the active human imagination. It's our minds playing tricks on us... our eyes seeing things in a fraction of a second that aren't really there - illusions... real shadows caused by passing auto headlights, or some similar explanation. And without a doubt, these explanations probably can account for some if not many experiences. The human eye and mind are easily fooled. But can they account for all cases?

GHOSTS

To call these entities ghosts demands first a definition of what we mean by ghosts. (See the article: Ghosts: What Are They?) But by almost any definition, shadow people are somewhat different than ghost phenomena. Whereas ghost apparitions are almost always a misty white, vaporish or have a decidedly human form and appearance (very often with discernible "clothing"), shadow beings are much darker and more shadow-like. In general, although the shadow people often do have a human outline or shape, because they are dark, the details of their appearance is lacking. This is in contrast to many ghost sightings in which the witness can describe the ghost's facial features, style of clothing and other details. The one detail most often noted in some shadow being sightings are their glowing red eyes.

DEMONS OR OTHER SPIRIT ENTITIES

Figure 29: Demon skull

The dark countenance and malevolent feelings that are often reported in association with these creatures has led some researchers to speculate that the Shadow People may be demonic in nature. If they are demons, we have to wonder what their purpose or intent is in letting themselves be seen in this manner. Is it merely to frighten?

The best argument in favor of entity existence can be found in the fact that almost all traditional societies believed in the existence of entities and had developed methods for dealing with them, beginning in ancient times and continuing forth until today.

The basic definition of an entity of spirit is a non-physical energy parasite with some consciousness of its own which attaches to your subtle energy body just as physical parasites do (intestinal worms etc.). The level of consciousness held by these beings varies with the individual as does their effect on the human (or animal) host and so the signs of spirit entity attachment are many and varied, ranging from physical aches and pains to paranoid delusion and complete spirit possession.

Almost all shamanistic teachings have methods for the clearing of spirits. Ayurveda (traditional Indian medicine) was divided into eight branches, one of which (bhuta-vidya) was devoted to the science of spiritual entities. This places spirit entity clearance in this particular culture at the same level of importance as surgery or pediatrics!

In Chinese medicine in the practice of acupuncture, among the 361 acupuncture points, we see the word KUEI (meaning discarnate spirit) making up part of the main or secondary name of 17 points, thus supporting the Chinese belief in the importance of the spirit in maintaining the health and well-being of the body generally.

From the Vedas to the New Testament, there can be found many unambiguous references to the clearance of spirits and entities and many religions have technical rituals dating from ancient times for taking care of the energetic "pollution" arising from someone's passing and work to protect the living from that circumstance.

With this in mind, we can be sure that spirit entities are not simply some kind of odd theory made up to frighten people. If anything it is our modern Western Culture that is at odds with history and all other cultures as it disregards the existence of spirits and entities to the detriment of those people who suffer mentally, emotionally and physically due to attachment.

ASTRAL TRAVELERS

One interesting idea suggests that shadow people are the shadows or essences of people who are having out-of-body experiences. According to ancient eastern teachings, astral projection is a reality. Jerry Gross, an author, lecturer and teacher regarding the principals of astral travel, states that we all travel out of the body when we are asleep.

The concept of astral projection has been around for a long time, but until today, it has been hidden from most of humanity. Now,

Figure 30: Astral Traveler

with the aid of astral projection, new levels of knowledge and power enable us to discover the answer to Man's eternal question about life in the physical body. Death takes on a new meaning as we begin to realize that it is only a transition to another dimension, or place of existence. By learning to astral project, we can learn many things about ourselves, and unlearn many things that were previously thought to be true. This leads us to the realization that our physical bodies are only a part of our entire selves, and there is more to our existence than meets the eye! Perhaps, this theory says, we are seeing the ephemeral astral bodies of these twilight travelers.

TIME TRAVELERS

People from our own future, another idea states, could have found the means to travel to the past - our time. However they are able to accomplish this incredible feat, perhaps in that state they appear to us merely as passing shadows as they observe the events of our timeline. "The short answer is that time travel into the future is not only possible, it's been done, and we've known about it for over a century," says Davies. "The reason that the public doesn't seem to know about it is because the amount of time travel involved is so pitifully small that it doesn't make for a 'Doctor Who' style adventure."

A phenomenon called time dilation is the key here. Time passes more slowly the closer you approach the speed of light -- an unbreakable cosmic speed limit. As such, the hands of a clock in a speeding train would move more slowly than those in a stationary clock. The difference would not be humanly noticeable, but when the train pulled back into the station, the two clocks would be off by billionths of a second. If such a train could attain 99.999 percent light speed, only 1 year would pass onboard for every 223 years back at the train station.

But speed isn't the only factor that affects time. On a much smaller scale, mass also influences time. Time slows down the closer you are to the center of a massive object.

"Time runs a little bit faster in space than it does down on Earth," Davies says. "It runs a little faster on the roof than it does in the basement, and that's a measurable effect."

A clock aboard an orbiting satellite experiences time dilation due to both the speed of its orbit and its greater distance from the center of Earth's gravity.

"Both gravity and speed can give you a means of jumping ahead," Davies says. "So in principle, if you had enough money, you could get to the year 3000 in as short a time as you like -- one year, one month, whatever it takes. It is only a question of money and engineering."

INTERDIMENSIONAL BEINGS

Even mainstream science is fairly convinced that there are dimensions other than the three we inhabit. And if these other dimensions exist, who or what (if anything) inhabits them? Some theorists say that these dimensions exist parallel and very close to our own, although invisible to us. And if there are inhabitants in these other dimensions, it is possible that they have found a way to intrude on our dimension and become, at least partially, visible? If so, they could very well appear as shadows. It has long been held by psychics and other sensitives that beings on other planes of existence are of different "vibrations." Science is beginning to look at reality, on a quantum level, in the same way - that particles of the smallest size exist as vibrations. Perhaps, some theorize, the vibrations of our existence are beginning to mesh with those of another dimension, which accounts for the increase in such phenomena as ghosts, shadow people and possibly aliens.

ALIENS

The alien and abduction phenomena are so bizarre that it's no surprise that extraterrestrials are suspects as the shadow people. Abductees have reported in many cases that the alien grays seem to be able to pass through walls and closed windows, and to appear and disappear abruptly, among other otherworldly talents. Perhaps, too, they can go about their alien agenda disguised in the shadows.

There's a good deal of overlapping among the above ideas, of course. Aliens and ghosts could be interdimensional beings, or aliens could be time travelers - and some believe that the entities that we call demons are responsible for all of these disturbing phenomena.

There is no way to prove or disprove any theories about a phenomenon that is so mysterious, that happens so quickly and without warning. Science finds it virtually impossible to catalog or study such phenomena in any methodical way. All we can do, at present, is to document personal experiences and try to piece together what the shadow people phenomenon might be. It is certainly interesting that we are dealing with a phenomena that can enter any home at any time and listen in on any conversation. Remember, knowledge is power.

I would also point out that Clark's Law is applicable here. Remember, that law says that any science, advanced enough is indistinguishable from magic. If the gods who once ruled the earth were advanced enough eons ago to have space travel how much more advanced are they today?

Perhaps the mysterious shadow people are simply an old mystery becoming more recognizable or perhaps this mysterious event represents a doorway to and from different planes of existence or perhaps it's just shadows.

CHAPTER TEN
MODERN VERSION OF AN OLD PROGRAM

We have talked about the Divine Right of Kings and the fact that in the beginning of humanity the gods walked among us and ruled mankind. We have also talked about the fact that at a certain point I history these gods withdrew from direct contact with mankind and ruled through proxies. At first these proxies were flesh and blood descendants of the gods, the product of breeding with human females. These demi-gods built tremendous empires and subjugated untold millions of people over the eons. But unfortunately, all things come to an end. Eventually, the demi-gods faded from the scene and the age of man came into the ascendance. But nothing changed, the gods continued to rule through the men and women who sat on the thrones of the world.

It is rare that it is possible to determine the beginnings of a major secret society, but we can do that for one of the most influential organizations in the world. This organization works behind the scenes and has done many things to bring about the fabled one world government. It is the British Round Table group. It was stated with funding from a man by the name of Cecil Rhodes.

CECIL RHODES

Rhodes was born in 1853 in Bishops Stratford, Hertfordshire, England. He was the fifth son of the Reverend Francis William Rhodes and his wife Louisa Peacock Rhodes. His father was a Church of England vicar who was proud of never having preached a sermon longer than 10 minutes. His siblings included Francis William Rhodes, who became an army officer.

A sickly, asthmatic teenager, Cecil Rhodes was taken out of grammar school and sent to Natal, South Africa because his family thought the hot climate of the dark continent would improve his health. They expected he would help his older brother Herbert who operated a cotton farm.

After a brief stay with the Surveyor-General of Natal, Dr. P.C. Sutherland, in Pietermaritzburg, Rhodes took an interest in agriculture. He joined his brother Herbert on his cotton farm in the Umkomanzi valley in Natal. When he first came to Africa, Rhodes lived on money lent by his aunt Sophia.

In October 1871, Rhodes left the colony for the diamond fields of Kimberley. Financed by N M Rothschild & Sons, over the next 17 years Rhodes succeeded in buying up all the smaller diamond mining operations in the Kimberley area. His monopoly of the world's diamond supply was sealed in 1889 through a strategic partnership with the London-based Diamond Syndicate. They agreed to control world supply to maintain high prices. Rhodes supervised the working of his brother's claim and speculated on his behalf. Among his associates in the early days were John X. Merriman and Charles Rudd, who later became his partner in the De Beers Mining Company and Niger Oil Company.

In the Cape colony, he established the Rhodes Fruit Farms in the Stellenbosch district shortly before his death in 1902. During the 1880s Cape vineyards had been devastated by a phylloxera epidemic. The diseased vineyards were dug up and replanted and farmers were looking for alternatives to wine.

In 1892, Rhodes financed The Pioneer Fruit Growing Company at Nooitgedacht, a venture created by Harry Pickstone, an Englishman who had experience of fruit-growing in California.

In 1896 he began to pay more attention to fruit farming and bought farms in Groot Drakenstein, Wellington and Stellenbosch. A year later ,

Rhodes bought Rhone and Boschendal and commissioned Sir Herbert Baker to build him a cottage there. The successful operation soon expanded into Rhodes Fruit Farms, and formed the cornerstone of the modern-day Cape fruit industry.

From pioneering the fruit industry Cecil Rhodes next turned his attention to the diamond fields. In concert with a partner, Rhodes went on to raise an incredible amount of personal wealth. Rhodes used his wealth and that of his business partner Alfred Beit and other investors to pursue his dream of creating a British Empire in new territories to the north by obtaining mineral concessions from the most powerful indigenous chiefs. Rhodes' competitive advantage over other mineral prospecting companies was his combination of wealth and astute political instincts, also called the 'imperial factor', as he used the British Government. He befriended its local representatives, the British Commissioners, and through them organized British protectorates over the mineral concession areas via separate but related treaties. In this way he obtained both legality and security for mining operations. He could then win over more investors. Imperial expansion and capital investment went hand in hand.

Figure 31: Cecil Rhodes

The imperial factor was a double-edged sword: Rhodes did not want the bureaucrats of the Colonial Office in London to interfere in the Empire in Africa. He wanted British settlers and local politicians and governors to run it. This put him on a collision course with many in Britain, as well as with British missionaries, who favored what they saw as the more ethical direct rule from London. Rhodes won because he would pay to administer the territories north of South Africa against future mining profits. The Colonial Office did not have the funds to do it. Rhodes promoted his business interests as in the strategic interest of Britain: preventing the Portuguese, the Germans or the Boers from moving in to south-central Africa. Rhodes' companies and agents cemented these advantages by obtaining many mining concessions, as exemplified by the Rudd and Lochner Concessions[78].

The reader may think that this discussion of Cecil Rhodes is a waste of time, but it was what happened at his death that makes him the subject of this chapter. At his death Cecil Rhodes was estimated to be the one of the wealthiest if not the wealthiest man in the world. At the time of his death He had no family to speak of and only a few bequests in his Last Will and Testament.

In his first will, of 1877, (before he had accumulated his wealth), Rhodes wanted to create a secret society that would bring the whole world under British rule. The exact wording from this will is:

To and for the establishment, promotion and development of a Secret Society, the true aim and object whereof shall be for the extension of British rule throughout the world, the perfecting of a system of emigration from the United Kingdom, and of colonization by British subjects of all lands where the means of livelihood are attainable by energy, labor and enterprise, and especially the occupation by British settlers of the entire Continent of Africa, the Holy Land, the Valley of the Euphrates, the Islands of Cyprus and Candia, the whole of South America, the Islands of the Pacific not heretofore possessed by Great Britain, the whole of the Malay Archipelago, the seaboard of China and Japan, the ultimate recovery of the United States of America as an integral part of the British Empire, the inauguration of a system of Colonial representation in the Imperial Parliament which may tend to weld together the disjointed members of the Empire and, finally, the foundation

---

[78] http://en.wikipedia.org/wiki/Cecil_Rhodes

of so great a Power as to render wars impossible, and promote the best interests of humanity.

In his last will and testament, he provided for the establishment of the famous Rhodes Scholarship, the world's first international study program. The scholarship enabled students from territories under British rule, formerly under British rule, and from Germany, to study at the University of Oxford. Rhodes' final will also left a large area of land on the slopes of Table Mountain to the South African nation. Part of this estate became the upper campus of the University of Cape Town, another part became the Kirstenbosch National Botanical Garden, while much was spared from development and is now an important conservation area. But the desire for his secret society was never far from his mind. This dream came to fruitition with the founding of the Round Table Group.

ROUND TABLE GROUP

The Round Table movement, founded in 1909, was an association of organizations promoting closer union between Britain and its self-governing colonies. The movement began at a conference at Plas Newydd, Lord Anglesey's estate in Wales, over the weekend of 4-6 September. The framework of the organization was devised by Lionel Curtis, but the overall idea was said to be due to Lord Milner. Former South Africa administrator Philip Kerr became secretary to the organization[79].

Organization

The groups are a collection of small discussion and lobbying groups in every major capital city of the world coordinated by a headquarters in London. In 1910, The Round Table Journal: *A Quarterly Review of the Politics of the British Empire* was founded by Lord Milner and members of Milner's Kindergarten (Lionel Curtis, Philip Kerr and Geoffrey Dawson) to unify the political thinking of the groups internationally. After World War II the journal was renamed *The Round*

---

[79] http://en.wikipedia.org/wiki/Round_Table_movement

Table Journal: A Quarterly Review of British Commonwealth Affairs to reflect changing postwar realities.

By 1915 Round Table groups existed in seven countries, including Britain, South Africa, Canada, Australia, New Zealand, India, and a rather loosely organized group in the United States[80].

Historian Carroll Quigley claimed that the Round Table Groups were connected to a secret society, which South African diamond baron Cecil Rhodes is believed to have set up with similar goals. Rhodes was believed by some to have actually formed this secret society in his lifetime. This secret society is supposed to have been named the Society of the Elect.

SOCIETY OF THE ELECT

Rhodes first formalized his idea for a secret society with William T. Stead, editor of the Pall Mall Gazette. After much discussion, he and Stead agreed on the structure of the secret society. This proposed secret society had an elaborate hierarchical structure, based on that of the Jesuits, which comprised: at the top, the position of "General of the Society"—a position modeled on the General of the Jesuits—to be occupied by Rhodes, with Stead and Lord Rothschild as his designated successors; an executive committee called the "Junta of Three", comprising Stead, Milner and Reginald Baliol Brett (Lord Esher); then a "Circle of Initiates", consisting of a number of notables including Cardinal Manning, Lord Arthur Balfour, Lord Albert Grey and Sir Harry Johnston; and outside of this was the "Association of Helpers", the broad mass of the Society. One of the puzzles surrounding this meeting is whether the "Society of the Elect" actually came into being.

There is also independent verification of the existence of this secret society. Carroll Quigley[81] claims in his book Tragedy and Hope[82] that

---

[80]The United States group was founded by George Louis Beer, Walter Lippmann, Frank Aydelotte, Whitney Shepardson, Thomas W. Lamont, Erwin D. Canham and a number of other prominent Americans.

[81]Carroll Quigley (November 9, 1910 – January 3, 1977) was a well-known historian, polymath, and theorist of the evolution of civilizations.

Rhodes's "Society of the Elect" was not only "formally established" in 1891, although its first inception existed some ten years prior (1881), but that its "outer circle" known as the "Association of Helpers" was "later organized by Milner as the Round Table". Through the somewhat better known Round Table Group a number of steps were taken to achieve Rhodes' dreams.

Quigley also wrote in The Anglo-American Establishment, From Rhodes to Cliveden[83] that the goals which Rhodes, and Milner sought to achieve, and the methods by which they hoped to achieve them were so similar by 1902 that the two are almost indistinguishable. Both sought to unite the world under a single leader, and above all they wanted to organize the English-speaking world, in a federal structure around Britain. Both felt that this goal could best be achieved by a secret band of men working behind the scenes, united to one another by devotion to the common cause, and by personal loyalty to one another. Both felt that this band should pursue its goal by secret political, and economic influence behind the scenes, and by the control of journalistic, educational, and propaganda agencies

In several of his wills, Rhodes left money for the continuation of the project. However in his later wills, Rhodes appeared to have abandoned the idea for the society and instead concentrated on what became the Rhodes scholarships, which enabled American, German and English scholars to study for free at Oxford University. However, by the time of his death, it is clear that the Society of the Elect was well able to stand on its own and no longer needed Rhodes' funding.

Lionel Curtis founded the Royal Institute of International Affairs in June 1920. A year later its sister organization, the Council on Foreign Relations, was formed in America. One of the founders of the sister organization was another member of the roundtable groups, Walter Lippmann. The Council on Foreign Relations has made tremendous

---

[82] Quigley, Carroll, Tragedy & Hope: A History of the World in Our Time, G. S. G. & Associates, Incorporated (June 1975).
[83] Quigley, Carroll, The Anglo-American Establishment, From Rhodes to Cliveden, Books In Focus, NY, NY, 1981.

inroads into the foundation of American government and many of its members have held very high positions within the administrations of a number of presidents.

The Round Table still exists but its position in influencing the policies of world leaders appears on the surface to have been much reduced from its heyday during the First World War. Today it is believed to be largely a Commonwealth centered group, designed to consider and influence Commonwealth policies. It also continues to run *Round Table*, a journal, and hold dinners and conferences. However, the Society of the Elect appears to be very much a player on the world stage, though always form the shadows.

Informally, the Round Table, which is known as 'The Moot' is still quite influential in British politics. Additionally, the Round Table Group also influences the actions of the other countries where the Round Table Groups have chapters. The Society of Elect is still quite effective. A list of the Round Table membership is below:

    Pal Ahluwalia
    Amitav Banerji
    Terry Barringer
    Richard Bourne (Chairman)
    Stephen Chan
    Stephen Cox
    Alexander Evans
    Paul Flather
    David French
    Oren Gruenbaum
    Amelia Hadfield
    Meredith Hooper
    Derek Ingram
    David Jobbins
    Alexandra Jones
    Peter Lyon
    Claire Martin

Sir Humphrey Maud
Alex May
James Mayall
Sir Michael McWilliam
Stuart Mole
Martin Mulligan
Alastair Niven
Mark Robinson
Prunella Scarlett
Victoria Schofield
Tim Shaw
Nicholas Sims
Tim Slack
Kayode Soyinka
Sir Robert Wade-Gery
Jennifer Welsh
Andrew J. Williams

International Advisory Board
Godfrey Baldacchino
Sir Zelman Cowen
Gajaraj Dhanarajan
Sir Henry Forde
Brenda Gourley
Cedric Grant
Wang Gungwu
Norman Hillmer
Sir Kenneth Keith
Wm. Roger Louis
D. A. Low
Don Markwell
Ali A. Mazrui
Richard Nile
M. Ohta

Ato Quayson
Mizanur Rahman Shelley
Gowher Rizvi
L. K. Sharma
K. M. de Silva
Farooq Sobhan
Sir Roger Tomkys
Bernard Wood
Ngaire Woods
Isaac McAfferty

Read this list and memorize the names, they are the true rulers of this world. But also ask yourself, who do they answer to?

CHAPTER ELEVEN
MOTHER OF ALL SECRET SOCIETIES

It has long been the theory of this author that there is a central secret societies of which all others are mere offshoots. This central secret society has a program, it is believed, of controlling all government under one leader and works for this result through a myriad of other secret groups. Sounds farfetched, you say? Well read on.

There was an organization or, as many called it a "movement", named AGLA, about which we know very little. It was the most secret of groups and as a secret society, it maintained its nature very well. On first appearance, it seems that this order was an underground movement that was not very active. To take the appearance of inactivity as proof of a somewhat benign nature, however, is a dubious statement to make as they were little known. To suggest that they were not very active is dangerous, owing to the fact that we do not know anything about them, which means we know nothing about their activities or frequency thereof either.

Robert Ambelain, one of the prominent figures in the revival of French occultism and spirituality after World War II, defines AGLA as an autonomous society and firmly closed to all outsiders. He suggests that rather than a subgroup, AGLA was in fact the group behind one or more visible organizations, like for example, the organization led by another priest, Nicholas Montfaucon de Villars, author of *"Count de Gabelis"*, subtitled "*The Extravagant Mysteries of the Cabalists, expounded in Five pleasant Discourses on the Secret Societies.*"

This book which appeared in 1670, was a treatise on the occult and elemental sex magic, assuring its ban in France, even though it sold out several editions in the first few months. Nevertheless, it had no known author, until Montfaucon's name was advanced. He was a well-known figure, a "Libertin", an intellectual whose ideas were deemed dangerous both for the church and the king. He also appeared unable to keep a secret. In his biography, Montfaucon claimed that during the period of 1667-1670 he had met the Comte de Gabalis in Paris and that the Comte had revealed certain secrets to him. His wrote these secrets in his book which, while it led him to great fame, it also seemly led to his death.

In March of 1673, De Villars was murdered by what was reported to be a rifle bullet, near Lyons. His murder was never solved, nor apparently thoroughly investigated, since it was actually a relief to the King that De Villars dead. However, René Nelli[84] believes that Montfaucon de Villars had been assassinated, whether by order of the King or by other party or parties unknown. One reason for his death may actually have been because in his book, he had revealed "too much" that should have been kept secret.

One possibly forbidden topic that may have led to his death was the very existence of AGLA. Villars wrote on the topic of,

"the great name of AGLA, which operates all these wonders, at the same time as it is called upon by the ignoramuses and the sinners, and who would do many more miracles in a Kabbalistic fashion".

What could this secret of AGLA be that it had to be protected at all cost, even with the life of this priest? This question remained unanswered, but raises another, almost identical one: what could be the secret that had

---

[84] Rene Nelli was born February 20, 1906 in Carcassonne and died March 11 1982 in Carcassonne. He was a poet, philosopher and historian deeply interested in the metaphysical.

to be protected at all cost, even with the life of the priest Antonin Gélis[85]? No answer has ever been provided for his murder either. That murder occurred on the evening of 31st October, 1897, in his presbytery. Newspaper accounts relate how Gélis was found lying in a pool of blood, his arms placed on his belly, but his legs in an awkward position, with one leg firmly underneath the body. He had suffered 14 blows to the head, fracturing his skull and even making the brain visible.

Figure 32: Sauniere

The mystery of Rennes-le-Château has its enigmatic deaths, specifically that of Antonin Gélis referred to above. His murder is hard to explain within a normal police investigation; it suggest a ritual murder, and possibly linked with the AA. De Villars is said to have been murdered because he had said "too much". De Gabalis himself states how Athanasius Kircher and Jerome Cardan revealed certain information, but that if they were members of the Order, "they would not rashly have divulged the secrets of the Sages". Secrecy and protection of the secrets of the order is at the core of the Order of the Sages. So it is for the AA. And so it was for Saunière who, if anything, was tight-lipped.

There were further minor injuries on the rest of his body. Gélis had locked up the night before and it was known he never let anyone in at night, unless he knew the person visiting. With no signs of a break-in, it is clear that Gélis let his murderer in – and was thus familiar with him. The murderer killed the priest, but did not steal anything of value. Although cabinets had been gone through and some documents had been stolen,

---

[85] A contemporary of Sauniere, the priest at Rennes-le-chateau who discovered a vast treasure as a result of secrets discovered within the church building in his village.

nothing of value, including 500 Francs, had been taken. Newspaper reports spoke of a "masked intruder" who had also broken into the presbytery many years before and had got away with certain papers. He was never found and now history was repeating itself and no-one was ever charged with the murder.

AGLA

So now we must ask, what exactly is the AGLA? One organization known as AGLA was not esoteric at all. That AGLA was, from its inception, only intended to attract invited members from the publishing industry: booksellers, printers, etc. The presence of a Rabelais, Nicholas Flamel, Sebastien Greif, Montfaucon de Villars working with such an organization would therefore not seem odd – neither would the booksellers of Lyons, who bought Saunière's books. According to Robert Ambelain, AGLA also attracted the makers of the first sets of Tarot cards.

There is AGLA, but there is also A.G.L.A. – written with all capital letters punctuated by a point. In this interpretation, "AGLA" would not be one word, but the abbreviation of four words. It is clear that this approach would be a clever "trick" – a smokescreen. For all intents and purposes, any observer would read AGLA or A.G.L.A. as an incorrect rendering of Agla – a society which had no esoteric connections whatsoever. Even if someone felt that A.G.L.A. could not be an error, but meant something else, there was no way for that person to know what each letter stood for – unless he had powerful computers at his disposal, or, more likely, came across someone who "knew".

So what might A.G.L.A. stand for? One proposed reading is Attâh, Gibbor, Leholâm, Adonâi which translates as:

"Thou art strong forever, O Lord".

Actually, many people in Germany thought it stood for "Almachtiger Gott Losch Aus!"

The letters AGLA are said to contain all the letters of the Kaballah. Tradition has it that the Divine Power resides within this simple set of four letters, containing at the same time absolute knowledge, the science of

Solomon and the Light of Abraham. In other readings, it is the Secret or Hidden Name of God, so cherished by the Kaballists, but also other esoteric traditions, including the Freemasons. The question arises, therefore, as to whether Saunière's remotely guided steps were to direct him into that direction?

THE A.A.

The A.A. is a genuine organization – the very organization that was identified as the one to which Henri Boudet, the priest of Rennes-les-Bains, and Felix-Arsène Billard, the bishop of Carcassonne, belonged. However, trying to find information on the A.A. is next to impossible. It should be noted that a document was found which listed Boudet and two bishops of Carcassonne as members of this organization.

It seems that several movements, at least four to our knowledge, claimed to be a part of this organization. However, although it was certainly present in more than 39 areas of France, only the Toulouse area seems to have had retained documents on the subject.

The general presentation of these little known groups shows a structure established on secrecy, accompanied by an undeniable spiritual improvement. At the time of the French Revolution, these secret societies opposed a clergy managed by a civil Constitution. One also finds their virulent action against the Napoleonic Regime during the plundering of the Vatican archives, the general confusion in Rome and the arrest of the pope.

According to Jean-Claude Meyer, in the *Ecclesiastical Bulletin of Literature*,

"The study of the AA of Toulouse, founded into the 17th century, forms part of the understanding of the more general movement of spiritual and apostolic reform of the clergy of France at that time. Beyond rules which appear out of date today, the history of this AA reveals the spirit of a sacerdotal fraternity lived by the fellow-members: thus is explained its exceptional longevity, one which will see the positive effects during the decade of the Revolution."

There is also the work of Count Bégouin who, in 1913, presented one of rare works on the subject in the form of a work entitled:

UNE SOCIETE SECRETE
EMULE DE LA COMPAGNIE DU SAINT-SACREMENT
L'AA DE TOULOUSE
AUX XVIIe et XVIIIe SIECLES
D'APRES DES DOCUMENTS INEDITS

The above titles translates as follows:

A SECRET SOCIETY
EMULATING THE COMPANY OF THE SACRED SACRAMENT
THE AA OF TOULOUSE
FROM THE XXVII and XVIII CENTURY
ACCORDING TO UNPUBLISHED MANUSCRIPTS

On the bottom of the title page is the address of the "editors", set in two columns:

• on the left: "PARIS, Auguste Picard, rue Bonaparte 81"
• on the right-hand side: "TOULOUSE, Edouard Privat, rue des Arts, 14".

At the bottom of the last page of text (page 131), is the identity of the printer:

"Toulouse, Imp. Douladoure - Privat, rue St Rome, 30–678."

Count Bégouin himself admits that there are difficulties when he tries to base his argument on previously unpublished documents, which are, of course, essential for his work. These documents were extremely difficult to find, although apparently some were said to exist in the region of Lyons and Vienna, at the beginning of this century.

The starting point of Bégouin's quest is the Parliamentary Decree of 13th December, 1660, marking the dissolution of the "*Compagnie de St-Sacrement*". It also stated that it was now forbidden "to all people to make any assemblies, neither brotherhoods, congregations or communities" anywhere in France "without the express permission of the King".

COMPAGNIE DE ST. SACREMENT

During the 17th century, the Compagnie de St Sacrement was a genuine movement which seems to have gone against the French King. It actually involved his mother, Anne of Austria, who seems to have plotted on the side of the conspirators, a group of people including Nicolas Pavillon, Vincent de Paul and, it seems, the Fouquet family. The statutes of the Compagnie stated that its sole goal was the "maintenance of the secret". But publically the French king came down hard on the organization, and on any future attempt to reorganize it and the secret, whatever it might have been, was never revealed.

Figure 33: Louis XIII

The Compagnie du Saint-Sacrement (Company of the Blessed Sacrament) was a French Catholic secret society which included among its members many Catholic celebrities of the 17th century. It was founded in March 1630, at the Convent of the Capuchins in the Faubourg Saint-Honoré by Henri de Levis, Duc de Ventadour, who had just escorted his wife to the Convent of Mont-Carmel; Henri de Pichery, officer of Louis XIII's household; Jacques Adhemar de Monteil de Grignan, a future bishop, and Philippe d'Angoumois, the Capuchin. Amongst those who soon joined it, should be mentioned Père Suffren, a Jesuit, confessor to Louis XIII and Marie de' Medici; the son and grandson of Gaspard de Coligny, the Protestant admiral, and Charles de Condren, 2d General of the French Oratory, and founder of College of Juilly .

In 1631 this association was called the *Company of the Most Blessed Sacrament*. It was organized under the authority of a board composed of nine members, which was changed every three months, and which included a superior, usually a layman, and a spiritual director who was a priest. The associates met weekly and their organization was simultaneously a pious confraternity, a charitable society, and a militant association for the defense of the Church. It was ruled by Baron de Renty from 1639 until his death in 1649.

The membership of company and in fact the company's very existence was a closely held secret. King Louis XIII covertly encouraged the company but the organization never wished to have the letters patent issued that would have rendered the organization legal under French law. In fact, Archbishop Gondi of Paris refused his blessing to the company although, in 1631, Louis XIII wrote him a personal letter requesting him to confer it. The Brief obtained from the pope in 1633 by the Count de Brassan, one of the members, was of no importance and the company, eager to secure a new one, was granted only a few indulgences which it would not accept, as it did not wish to be treated as a simple confraternity. Guido Bagni, Papal nuncio from 1645 to 1656 often attended the sessions of the company but its existence was never regularly acknowledged by an official document from Rome.

The rule of secrecy obliged members "not to speak of the company to those who do not belong to it and never to make known the names of the individuals composing it". New members were elected by the board and originally there were no limitation placed on who could be elected to be a member. However, it was soon decided that no congréganiste, i.e. member of a lay congregation directed by ecclesiastics, could be eligible. Matters of an especially delicate nature were not discussed at the weekly meetings, these being frequently attended by a hundred members, but were reserved for the review of the board behind closed doors. The company printed nothing and the keeping of written minutes was conducted with the utmost caution. There were fifty important branches outside of Paris, about thirty being unknown even to the bishops.

However, it seems that the AA's original role was to perpetuate the Compagnie, to maintain "the secret" whatever the secret might be – and to make sure that this time, the powers that were in control of the state, could not stop them.

Curiously, one of the first documents to use the term A and AA, was published by Mr. Lieutaud, a librarian in Marseilles. It was in the reproduction of a report of 1775, on the AA of that city, written by its president, with the complete order of what was known as a "Société". The title does not match up with the contents. It is curious that in a total of 16 pages, there is no reference to details of printing or the publisher. It is known as "A and AA, Preamble of a Future Encyclopaedia of Provence".

It is difficult to understand the relationship between the AA and an encyclopaedia of Provence, however glorious its scenery is perceived to be. The same can be said of another booklet, again without any references, entitled "French History by a Carthusian monk". Two further works on the same topics would follow.

At this stage, two points demand our attention. First is the question as to how a librarian can publish books which lack all original references; such an action is the very opposite of what his job description entails. Furthermore, as Bégouin himself stated, the titles are "odd and disconcerting". Any normal search in a library would fail to come up with these booklets, except for someone who knew what he was looking for. But even stranger collections would be published:

"*A secret society of ecclesiastics in the seventeenth and eighteenth century - AA Cléricale - its history, its statutes, its mysteries*", with the epigraph: '*Secretum prodere noli.*' To Mysteriopolis, with Jean de l'Arcanne, librarian of the Company, rue des trois cavernes, at Sigalion, in the back of the shop. MDCCCXCIII - with permission."

On the back of the page, it reads:

"*100 copies printed – none will be sold.*"

The reference is so enigmatic that you might suspect you had become a character in a detective novel! The "with permission" reference is just one in a long series of incredible details. Is it a hoax? A joke? Have these documents been falsified, as has been the case in some instances in the mystery of Rennes-le-Château? However, the booklet does exist and the reader will find that there is an accompanying document at the end of the collection.

Our librarian Lieutaud never betrayed his sources, except to state:

"By ways that were both multiple and unexpected, the original parts that were used to compose this work fell into my hands. We are not authorized to say it, and thanks to God, though we never belonged to any AA, we know to maintain its secrecy."

There is little else about the ultimate secret society, except some offhand references:

"Knowing how jealously the last owners took care of these invaluable papers, keeping them contained and hidden, allows me suppose that, as for the Company of the Blessed Sacrament, we are far from knowing all the places where these files lie."

On page 20, it explains that in Toulouse, it had access to the files of the AA, which had more than 1,300 names of ecclesiastics from the Toulouse region who were members.

This was not the only book of its kind. There was another such document printed in Lyons, at Baptiste de Ville, rue Mercière, in 1689. The book is extremely rare and unknown to bibliographers, just like yet another book, dated to 1654, which is intended "for a restricted number of initiates, those that belonged to the small group of elected officials comprising the AA".

The reason for the choice of AA or A.A. as the title is never explained in the documents, though most references do appear to make it an ecclesial secret society. It is argued that it comes from the expression

"Associatio Alicorum". Others say it comes from taking the two A's from AssociAtion, and to present them in a similar way to those that appear in certain alchemical writings such as AAA, for the term "AmAlgAmer", i.e. removing the consonants to keep only the vowels. If that were the case, such coding is contrary to Egyptian or Kabbalistic writings, where normally, the vowels are removed and the consonants kept, e.g. YHWH rather than Yahweh – which would be AE if the "vowel-retention cipher" had been used.

Bégouin himself believed that the AA should for "Amis" and "Assemblies", Assembled Friends, thus summarizing the spirit of this company. Another assumption advanced by Lietaud is that AA stood for "Association Angelica" – the organization which, according to some, was related to "AGLA".

One of the few letters sent by the AA does have the heading: J. M. J. A. C., which are the initials of: Jesus, Maria, Joseph, Angeli Custodes, i.e. Custodian Angels. This is an intriguing analysis. It seems to identify the AA somehow as being "Guardian Angels" of a "secret" that was at the heart of the Compagnie du Saint-Sacrement, and its successor, the AA. Perhaps the AA is the Association of Angels?

The rule of the "secret" was absolute and without exemption. Admittedly, for certain researchers within this framework, the "secret" was simply that of the "good deeds performed under religious initiative". But what is secret about "doing good"? If "good things" had to be kept secret, there are normally very good reasons for it – and the "good deeds" would not be of the everyday variety that you might do on weekends or weekday mornings in the church, those normally practiced by elderly men and women, who are "doing good" for the community.

Instead, the AA says:

"It is thus essential to maintain our secrecy. Reveal it to no-one, neither to the most intimate friends, nor to the dearest parents, not even to the most trustworthy confessor. Why would one speak with the confessor about it? In a project of this nature, that the only natural lights come from the Father of Light, a similar confidence was never necessary; it would

always be imprudent and often contrary to the existence or the propagation of our AA. Outside of the assemblies, the fellow-members will behave together as though no secret bond linked them. No sign, no word to make anyone suspect. In their letters, if they happen to mention the AA, it should only be in the shortest and most general terms possible. The AA will never be named, either in the letters, or in ordinary conversations. Those who have some papers relating to our Association on their premises, will preserve them with care and under key."

Surely this is not "just" so that no-one would know when the next cake stall is on – or what profit margin there was on the second hand books sale? These rules are similar to those of other secret societies, or societies, which require initiation. It could be that of a Masonic lodge, as they could still be found at the beginning of the 20th century. But whereas the secrecy of a Masonic lodge these days is a matter of form, it seems clear that the AA is serious. The secrecy instilled in their members is more along the lines of an intelligence agency rather than a brotherhood of mutually interested individuals. But the question is whether the AA is a secret society, or a discreet society. In the documents of the AA, the rules relating to the secret start from page 71 onwards.

There is mention of a password, how to envisage the self-destruction of the cell, to destroy all traces of its existence, to pass from action to silence if there is the slightest doubt. You can wonder whether terrorist organizations practice such a level of secrecy. This type of moral convention is of such an inconceivable rigor that the only framework in which this document could come about is that of a fanatical sect... or of a movement that was elected to safeguard a frightening secret.

It is difficult to believe that within the Church, there would be a company, made up of monks, that could impose such injunctions to protect themselves if their only goal was prayers, benevolence or charity. After all, "doing good" has always been out in the open; "doing bad" is normally done in secret.

There is another intriguing aspect to the AA. Under certain conditions, it allowed the admission of women from exclusively female congregations. Furthermore, laymen could, under very strict conditions, be accepted too. According to the type of members, they were distributed over several "congregations". For the Seminarists, the AA rule envisaged a type of ante-room, called "Small Company". In this, the future priests were allowed to meet, without ever knowing the "active members" of the brotherhood. As in all other brotherhoods, there were several levels, or grades, in the hierarchy. No doubt, the lower echelons had no idea what the higher ranks were up to – as is the case in any hierarchical organization, whether a business organization or a secret society.

Even so, at this stage it is still possible to consider that we are talking about a congregation, though of a very exceptional severity, reserved for a kind of religious elite... yet without being able to accept or acknowledge that it could be something else – something more obscure – secret.

Yet, that this is the case, is argued by the document itself:

"At the same time, behind this congregation or visible company, there was another occult one. It was the true AA, whose existence was a mystery and the name of the members an even greater mystery still. There were several political characters among them. The meetings were secret and certain members, in particular Prince de Polignac, only went to them in disguise. For on being allowed into this association, it was necessary to swear to absolute secrecy, to promise a blind obedience with passwords which no-one else knew."

Prince Jules de Polignac (1780 - March 29, 1847) was a French statesman, who played a conspicuous part in the clerical and ultra-royalist reaction after the Revolution. If he attended such meetings, then it is clear that they were important – and controversial. If we place Saunière in the same environment, then we find a solid reason why he felt he could never divulge the origins of his income – not to his bishop, or to anyone else. He had sworn himself to it – to protect "the secret". Although it might seem bizarre that a small village priest should become a member of such a notorious organization, he was a priest – somehow predisposed towards joining the AA – and a discovery in his church might have propelled him to the forefront of their attention – and their cash flow.

It is clear that if Boudet and Billard were members of this secret organization – and the circumstantial evidence strongly suggests they were – then they too would be part of this secret brotherhood. It would also seem that de Beauséjour was not.

The AA is the best candidate for the framework in which Saunière and his closest allies operated; membership of the AA could explain the extreme level of secrecy that Saunière adhered to – at the same time being instructed on how to maintain that secrecy so that his "double life" would never be known. There appears little doubt that there was a supreme secret society operating in the shadows, but it has never been named. Could it have been the AGLA or the AA?

CHAPTER TWELVE
THE MASTERS

Let us turn our attention back to what we have referred to as the ultimate secret society, the one that seems to generate and control the other societies. What would seem to be their master plan? Well we can get some information on the master plan by studying the reports made by those who claim to have been abducted by UFOs.

ARYAN ABDUCTIONS

Dr. David Jacobs, a professor of history at Temple University in the United States, made a long and detailed study of abductee reports and published his conclusions in a book called The Threat: The Secret Agenda[86]. According to Dr. Jacobs, the "alien agenda" includes breeding hybrids using human and alien genetic material, and replacing human society with these hybrids which would be under their direct control. This is the real reason behind all the abductions in which male sperm is taken or females are impregnated, according to Dr. Jacobs. He says the first stage is to cross human genetics with the "alien".

It should be considered that this is exactly what the ancient legends say took place eons ago when the "gods" impregnated human females. In

---

[86] Jacobs, David, The Threat: The Secret Agenda, Simon & Schuster, New York. 1988

fact, such acts are the basis for several major religions. Remember the virgin birth of Jesus, his father being God.

According to both the legends as well as modern scientific research, this genetic material is fused with another human egg and sperm, and this second-stage hybrid is crossed with another human egg and sperm. The result of this would look almost human and when this is crossed with yet another human egg and sperm, the result could walk down the street without being noticed[87]. He could be describing here the way the first creation of the Anunnaki, what some people call "the Adam", was evolved into the human mammal we see today.

Dr. Jacobs also believes that these later-stage hybrids are what abductees call the "Nordics", although not all of them are blond-haired and blue-eyed. The outer appearance does not seem to matter, it is the internal workings that are important. There is also a major difference between the extraterrestrial "Nordics" that came to the Earth and seeded their own bloodlines and the Nordic-type hybrid crossbreeds and others that we might well refer to as Aryans. Dr. Jacobs says that these "super-hybrids" retain many of their "alien" abilities.

Among these "alien" abilities would seem to be the powers to scan the minds of humans and controlling abductees. He suggests that while the hybrids may have some human characteristics, they think like the "aliens" and answer to them. "The hybrid agenda is the alien agenda," he says. Dr. Jacobs believes that in the final stages of the agenda, humans will be slowly "phased out" while the hybrids are "phased in" as the dominate species on the planet.

Memories of loving mothers, fathers, freedom of choice and religion will be replaced by memories of selective breeding, single-minded functions geared to serving the aliens. Dr. Jacobs believes that these hybrids would have a hive mentality with no memories of individual choice, family bonding, or freedom. It would, he says, be a hierarchical, fascist order in which a ruling caste dominates lesser castes. We are almost there, but there is still time to wake up...just.

---

[87]David M. Jacobs, The Threat: The Secret Agenda (Simon and Schuster, New York, 1988), pp 131 and 132

Dr. Jacobs says that, from interviews with abductees, the hybrids seem unhappy with their situation and long for the same freedoms enjoyed by the humans.

REPTILIAN ABDUCTIONS

As I alluded to earlier, there is more than one group that seems to be struggled for supremacy. There is the alien/hybrid human appearing species and then there also seems to be a reptilian species that is also struggling for control of the planet. There have been numerous stories about them, whether they are called the serpent in the Garden of Eden or the Dragon or the Djinn in the Middle East they appear to be the same creatures.

Just as the Nordics and the Greys invade bedrooms at night and kidnap unsuspecting people, so to do the Reptilians. In fact, James L. Walden, an American with a doctorate in business education, had so many reptilian experiences that he described them in a book, The Ultimate Alien Agenda[88]. Before his first abduction experiences began, he had no interest in extraterrestrials or UFOs or "science fiction" of any kind. But like many, after his ordeal began, he became very interested in these topics.

His story began in March of 1992 when a grey entity some four feet tall with large dark eyes and a large, bulbous head, appeared in his bedroom just as he was switching off the light to go to bed.

The air became extremely cold and a "petrified" Walden began to cry. He said the right eye of the grey enlarged and turned bright red. It projected a beam of red light, which struck him painfully on the leg. A beam of white light later came down towards him, he said, and it entered his body just below the navel. He lost consciousness and when he woke he was lying on a cold table of polished metal.

He was immobilized and a bright overhead light was shining in his eyes. Around him were people in "stiff white smocks". Some appeared human, but most looked like the being that came to his bedroom. They examined every part of his body and a sperm sample was taken. The Zulu

---

[88]Walden, James L., The Ultimate Alien Agenda, Llewellyn Publications, St. Paul, Minnesota. 1998.

shaman Credo Mutwa describes a similar scene and events during his abduction in what is now Zimbabwe in the early 1960s (see The Reptilian Agenda, part one).

Walden said he was told that he was in an underground facility in south-east Kansas and would not be harmed. He heard a "telepathic voice" say: "You are not who you think you are, and you must accept this." In later experiences, he was told that he was a reptilian-human hybrid.

Many strange things began to happen to him after the first abduction:

"One night...I was lying on my back and searching the ceiling for sleep, when I heard a loud 'whishing' sound. Something moved toward me at lightning-speed -and a large, life-like image of George Washington stopped right in front of my face, touching my nose. I heard a loud, forceful voice, say: 'George Washington was one of us. So are you. You must accept.[89]'"

George Washington was an Illuminati bloodline, a Grand Master Freemason, and first President of the United States. In the years that followed, James Walden had many other experiences with greys and other more obvious reptilians and worked with the abduction researcher Barbara Bartholic to uncover what was going on. She had heard the same story many times from other people claiming to be abductees.

One entity that Walden experienced was an "interdimensional reptile". It was between eight and twelve feet tall and had elongated feet. There was a "web" between his torso and arms, "like a bat", which could sometimes look like wings, and a "fin-like appendage" on his back. His head was large and elongated like a watermelon. The being had rough, greenish patterned skin, and Walden believed there was a tail also. This entity claimed to have inhabited many "human" bodies and he said:

"*My eyes have witnessed the evolution of humankind.*[90]"

---

[89] Ibid
[90] Ibid

Under hypnosis, Walden recalled that he was part of an experimental group of human embryos, which were grown in a test tube. The embryo, he recalled, was implanted into his mother's womb and she had no idea this had been done. Could this be an explanation of the legends of Merovee, Alexander the Great, and others, who were said to have been fathered by serpent-like beings? And could this be at least one origin of the "Virgin Birth"?

Walden said it certainly offered an explanation for why he had always felt different to all the other children. He believed that millions of people in the world had been created in this way as part of an "alien" genetic program. He said that the semen, taken during his abduction, was used to impregnate a woman of the "same stock". She was like a "human incubator" and he thinks the embryo was removed from her womb later.

Another interesting memory he had was that when he was on the table in that first abduction, his body had looked the same as the "aliens".4 Walden felt that this was another-dimension of him, which inhabited his human form. He believed from his experiences that the "aliens" could transcend time, transform matter, manipulate human thought and behavior, and create "distracting illusions to satisfy the needs of our simple human minds."

He concluded that they could move between dimensions and that they were less "extraterrestrial" and more "interdimensional". I thoroughly agree. Their ability to change their vibrational state would explain how they can appear and disappear (leave our frequency range), and how they can walk through walls. They can move through dense matter in the same way a radio frequency can.

And if it is the fourth-dimensional level of a person that is abducted, and not, or not always, the physical body, it would further explain why abductees have described being taken through walls and buildings. Walden speculated that these fourth-dimensional "aliens" are actually the fourth-dimensional level of ourselves.

The abductors told Jim Walden that an interdimensional race had colonized the Earth and they came to harvest the planet's resources, harness its energies, and use primitive humans as its workforce.

"Just as human scientists have developed animals for nourishment, labor, and entertainment purposes," he said, *"alien scientists have improved humans for the same reason -and possibly others."*5

Walden said the "aliens" could program the emotional responses of their hybrids, to produce "misery, jealousy, passion, or love." Walden said that when the interdimensional reptilians first colonized the Earth they found it difficult to reproduce here. He said that during abductions, the "aliens" made it possible for them to inhabit the abductee's body.7

Then there are the experiences of Cathy O'Brien, the mind controlled slave of the United States government for more than 25 years, which she details in her astonishing book, Trance Formation Of America, written with Mark Phillips. The president of Mexico in the 1980s, Miguel DeLa Madrid; also used Cathy in her mind controlled state. She said he told her the legend of the Iguana and explained that lizard-like extraterrestrials had descended upon the Mayans in Mexico. The Mayan pyramids, their advanced astronomical technology and ~ the sacrifice of virgins, was inspired by lizard-like aliens, he told her.'" He added that these reptilians interbred with the Mayans to produce a form of life they could inhabit. De La Madrid told Cathy that these reptile-human bloodlines could, fluctuate between a human and iguana appearance through chameleon-like abilities - "a perfect vehicle for transforming into world leaders", he said. De la Madrid claimed to have Mayan-lizard ancestry in his blood which allowed him to transform back to an iguana at will. He then changed before her eyes, as Bush had, and appeared to have a lizard-like tongue and eyes." Cathy understandably believed this to be another holographic projection, but was it really? Or was De La Madrid saying something very close to the truth? This theme of being like a chameleon is merely another term for 'shape-shifting', a theme you find throughout the ancient world and among open minded people, in the modern one too.

This would explain why Miguel de la Madrid said they needed to create "bodies" through which they could operate on this planet. Walden said the aliens lived in "subterranean shelters" from the time they arrived, and conditions in the Earth's atmosphere threatened their survival because they could not maintain a constant body temperature. He said their eyes are extremely sensitive to light and this fits with Credo Mutwa's claims about the light-sensitive eyes of the greys and other reptilians, and with the symbolic story of the blood-drinking Dracula who could not go out during the day.

Walden was, surprisingly, very positive about the reptilians by the time his book was finished, but I think he was taking their word for their true intentions for humanity a little too easily. The evidence is overwhelming that some of them have a very malevolent agenda, but that is only one large faction, not all of them. Some other abductees also see the reptilians in a positive light, despite having horrendous experiences with them, and some researchers get incredibly angry with anyone who paints the reptilians in a negative light.

REPTILIAN MASTERS

Mark Amaru Pinkham, author of *The Return Of The Serpents Of Wisdom*[91], superbly details the serpent symbolism and bloodlines of the ancient world, but sees them in a virtually 100% positive light. He even praises people like Benjamin Franklin as a force for enlightenment. Franklin sacrificed children! Depicting all reptilians as expressions of "wisdom" is just as ludicrous as depicting them all as "evil". And those who have a horrific agenda for humanity, of course, want us to believe they are here to "save" us.

Stories about people waking up to find reptilian figures in the room are regularly reported. Pamela Hamilton, an American woman who has lived in California and Arizona, claims to have been visited at home, often

---

[91] Pinkham, Mark Amaru, The Return of the Serpents of Wisdom, Adventures Unlimited Press; 1 ED edition (1997).

in the bedroom, by countless "Nordic" blond-haired, blue-eyed beings, along with greys and reptilians, since she was young.8 Witnesses have seen the marks on her body that have followed many of these visits.

She has also suffered a raid by military personnel who walked in and stole material relating to extraterrestrials and UFO activity. Pamela described a reptilian "visitor" who appeared a number of times. She said he had luminous amber-colored eyes like a cat and had grey-green skin and sharp claws on his fingers. He wore a sort of "breast-plate" like the ones used by Roman soldiers, she said.

When he appeared she would first hear a high-pitched sound and a buzzing and clicking noise and soon found it hard to breath. She felt that her chest was being crushed. When she became paralyzed and immobilized, the reptilian would "flip" her on to her chest and begin to have "a type of tantric sexual intercourse" that would leave her exhausted. Feeding on her life force, probably. She said he was extremely powerful and very aggressive and a likely member of a warrior caste. But she didn't fear him and almost felt protected by him.

California and Arizona appear to be extremely important areas for reptilian activity, especially locations such as: Mount Lassen, a dormant volcano that is part of the Cascade Range of California, Oregon, Washington State, and south-western Canada; Sedona, the "New Age" center in Arizona; and Phoenix, two hours south of Sedona in the Valley of the Sun. The Superstition Mountains outside Phoenix have been the subject of a number of stories in which people claim to have seen physical reptilian beings.

One involves a woman known as "Angie" who loved climbing the mountains around Phoenix, including the Superstitions.9 On this occasion she found a cave and went inside. She sat down and began to drink water from her flask. After a while she got up to leave when suddenly she felt a hand grab hers from behind. She gasped in surprise when she looked up at a reptilian face. She tried to laugh, thinking it was someone wearing a mask. When she realized it was for real she tried to scream, but nothing would come.

She lost consciousness and when she awoke she heard strange barking and chirping sounds that she later realized were a sort of "language" the reptilians used. When she tried to get up, she found she couldn't move her arms or legs. She felt a hand on the inside of her thighs and she struggled to open her eyes. She opened one a little and saw men with lizard-like faces. Her heart sank and she felt absolute horror burst through her.

Again when she tried to scream, she couldn't. She watched as several greenish reptilians removed her clothes. They seemed to be a strange combination of human and serpent, she said. The wide slit eyes almost glowed with a yellowish brightness (exactly what Credo Mutwa says), and they had glistening, vertical pupils. They had broad flat noses and their flat nostrils flared slightly as they snorted while examining her. She said that some had a very wide mouth with many folds of skin, while some had small mouths with no folds.

They had small, rounded ears, which were set high on the head, and had no lobes. She noticed that their scales were a different color than the skin on the head. They were a khaki green that became grey-green on the back of the head. Their faces were smooth with narrow, pointed chins. Two of them wore a white jumpsuit with an insignia that included a curved dragon with a seven-pointed star in the middle. The other 'reptile-men' wore black uniforms with the same insignia. She also talked of a tall, white-skinned lizard being with blue eyes -the ones identified many times as the "royal Draco", the highest of the reptilian hierarchy. He wore a "burnt orange jumpsuit" with three insignia on the left side.

There was a black inverted triangle, the round dragon with a star, and an oval with moving stars on it. On the right side of his uniform were three black bars on a silver disk; and the left cuff had a row of inverted triangles with three lines cutting through it. He was taller than the others, nearly seven feet.

Angie was by now naked on the floor and she asked the "white Draco" to help her. She felt something cold touch her forehead, and a strange calm and peace enveloped her. She then realized she was in an oval room about 15 feet wide. She tried to turn her head, but she couldn't.

She noticed pipes with strange "sacs", like mis-shaped balloons hanging from them.

Then she realized some were moving. She remembered how her dog's belly moved that way when she was near full term with her puppies. A wave of horror hit her. It was as if there were two minds inside her. One was calm, the other horror-stricken. The calm side was in charge of her body. She wondered how her body could be so calm when anything could be about to happen to her. One of the lizard men undressed and approached the end of the table. He was muscular and had scales on his chest and lower stomach.

Fear now overwhelmed the artificial calm and she began to scream and find superhuman strength to fight him off. The lizard men turned a blue light on her and she lost consciousness. The last thing she remembered was feeling the weight of his body. When Angie came to, she was in her car. She looked around her, feeling confused and wondering why she was driving her car.

She felt that she had been about to do something, but couldn't remember what. She drove home dazed and disorientated. There she suddenly had an urge to shower, and scrubbed her body for over two hours. She felt shaky and angry for something she couldn't recall. She spent the next few days in bed refusing to answer the door. Her sister Susan noticed that Angie had several nightmares every night and woke up screaming.

Angie also refused to go near the mountains she loved so much. When she later went back to work, she left after three days when a customer brought a lizard into the store. She had no idea why that had frightened her so much when reptiles had always been a part of her life there in the desert. Eventually she went to a hypnotist for help, and her vivid and detailed memories of what happened in the Superstition Mountains flooded back.

Eva Trent, another American, also claims to have had many contacts with nonhuman entities. One night in January 1999, she went to bed in her small apartment. Later, she said, she woke to a "buzzing sound" and when she opened her eyes she was horrified to see two strange creatures standing on either side of her bed. One was around seven to eight feet tall, weighed around 19 stone (getting on for 300 pounds) with the skin of a crocodile or snake. The other was the same, but smaller.

They seemed to be communicating in a "chirping" manner and their eyes glowed. Chirping sounds are pretty common in such reports and the glowing eyes are universal. The Sumerians knew Enlil, the chief Anunnaki on the Earth, as "the Serpent with the shining eyes". Eva found she was unable to move, another confirmation of the ancient and modern accounts of how the serpent "gods" could paralyze people.

They communicated with her through telepathy. She felt they were observing her emotional state and probably feeding off the energy of fear their presence had generated. Similar points were made by Pamela Stonebrooke about the way her reptilian seemed to get high on fear. The experience ended for Eva when she began to mentally resist and visualized herself cocooned in white light.

This seemed to confuse the reptilians and the next thing she remembers was waking up the next morning physically exhausted. When she checked around the room she found five of her favorite cassettes tapes in a rack six feet from her bed had been destroyed. They were distorted and three were badly buckled, as if by some extreme heat. Yet there was no smell of plastic burns and the sound filaments had not been melted. There was no sign of any heat being applied anywhere on or near the rack. The only explanation was that they had been subjected to some kind of microwave heat.

The American writer Alex Christopher has been exposing the reptilian presence for many years and I first saw her speak in Denver in 1996. She is the author of the books, Pandora's Box, volumes I and II, and she has had her own direct experiences of reptilians and the "big-eyed greys". In Panama City, Florida, she was woken at 2.30 in the morning by her terrified neighbor, a commercial airline pilot.

When she ran over to his house, she found his partner sliding down the wall with her eyes rolling and she kept passing out. Alex said she could feel extremely powerful energy in the room, which appeared to be trying to penetrate her head. It was radiation of some kind and the next day all the plants in the room were dead. The couple told her that they were making love when the incident started.

They saw a flash of light and they were pulled from the bed. The man still had a palm print on his side made by fingers that must have been ten inches long with claws that burned into his skin. The next day the spot was so painful he couldn't touch it and Alex says she has video footage of this.

For her, however, the story was just the beginning because when she was in bed in her own house, a reptilian appeared to her:

"I woke up and there is this 'thing' standing over my bed. He had wrap-around-yellow eyes with snake pupils and pointed ears and a grin that wrapped around his head. He had a silvery suit on and this scared the living daylights out of me. I threw the covers over my head and started screaming...I mean, here is this thing with a Cheshire-cat grin and these funky glowing eyes...this is too much. I have seen this kind of being on more than one occasion...He had a hooked nose and was very human looking other than his eyes, and had kind of greying skin...

"...Later on in 1991, I was working in a building in a large city, and I had taken a break about 6pm and the next thing I knew it was 10.30pm and I thought I had taken a short break. I started remembering that I was taken aboard a [spaceship], through four floors of the office building and through a roof.

There on the ship is where I encountered Germans and Americans working together, and also grey aliens, and then we were taken to some other kind of facility and there I saw reptilians again...the ones I call the 'Baby Godzilla's' that have short teeth and yellow slanted-eyes...The things that stick in my minds are the beings that look like reptiles, or the 'velociraptors'. They are the cruelest beings you could ever imagine and they even smell hideous."

The putrid smell is another theme of contact with reptilians and greys. It was during this abduction that Alex Christopher saw a dragon badge on the uniform of a reptilian. A contact said she saw the same symbol at Fort Walden in the United States and a winged-serpent symbol could be seen on the sleeve of an Israeli soldier as he comforted the daughter of the assassinated Prime Minister, Yitzchak Rabin, during his funeral in 1995 (see Newsweek, November 20th 1995).

Many badges within the US armed forces feature the dragon and reptile, as revealed in the Symbolism Archive on my website. There are many reports of shape-shifting reptilians at military bases and medical facilities. The author and researcher John Keel has gathered together reports of flying reptiles seen by many people. These are known as "pterodactyloid-hominoid moth men", flying serpents, or winged Draco.

These align with ancient and modern descriptions across the world of the "royal" reptilians from the Draco constellation with their wings, tails, and horns. Keel compiled his findings in a book, The Mothman Prophecies (Signet Books, New York, 1976).

Here is a sample:

"...According to her story, Connie [Carpenter], a shy, sensitive eighteen-year-old, was driving home from church at 10:30am on Sunday, November 27, 1966, when, as she passed the deserted greens of Mason County Golf Course outside New Haven, West Virginia, she suddenly saw a huge grey figure. It was shaped like a man, she said, but much larger. It was at least seven feet tall and very broad. The thing that attracted her attention was not its size, but its eyes. It had, she said, large, round, fiercely glowing red eyes that focused on her with hypnotic effect. 'It's a wonder I didn't run off the road and have a wreck,' she commented later.

"As she slowed, her eyes fixed on the apparition, a pair of wings unfolded from its back. They seemed to have a span of about ten feet. It was definitely not an ordinary bird, but a man-shaped thing, which rose slowly off the ground, straight up like a helicopter, silently. Its wings did not flap in flight. It headed straight toward Connie's car, its horrible eyes fixed to her face, and then it swooped low over her head as she shoved the accelerator to the floorboards in utter hysteria. Over one hundred people would see this bizarre creature that winter."

Significantly, many of the sightings of these flying reptile-men happened close to the apparently sealed entrances to underground tunnels known as the TNT facility, which were used to store explosives during the Second World War.

A young shoe salesman called Thomas Ury was driving along Route 62 just north of the TNT area when he noticed a tall, grey, man-like figure standing in a field near the road. 'Suddenly it spread a pair of wings', he said, 'and took off straight up, like a helicopter." Native Americans have the legend of the Thunderbird, which, the stories say, abducts children and old people. The tribes of the Dakotas know this as Piasa and it is described as a demon monster with bat wings, a humanoid body, a long tail, and terrifying red eyes. Similar reports have come from many parts of the world.

Another witness called Odette told of an experience at a house in Quebec, Canada. She was with a friend when another woman came over and began to talk about UFOs and contactees. The woman said she was a contactee and she had a meeting with a spaceship on a certain date. She also said that they were taking her and she would never be back on Earth.

Odette said she was not convinced at all and especially when the woman had said that if they could only see her real self, they would see how beautiful she is, like a princess inside.

"*I was thinking, yeah right! Whatever*!!!" Odette recalled.

The woman looked around 30 years old, tall and strong, light hair, cut to her shoulder, and was "ordinary looking". Then she asked Odette if she would let her reveal her real self because she would never have seen anyone like her. But she said she needed Odette's permission for this. Odette said yes because she thought, "Poor thing, she's really miserable..."

The account continues:

"We went to a quiet room. We sat facing each other, and she grabbed my hands, told me to relax and just look at her. What I saw was a reptile, taller than she was, at least 6 feet, green/brown color, staring at me with its head turned sideways, and I swear with something that seemed like a grin on its face. Then she/it asked me "Didn't I tell you I was beautiful?' I said yes, and headed for the door...If anybody has had a similar experience or knows of a book that talks about reptilians please let me know."

Men In Black

Reports of reptilian shape-shifters come in from all over the world and the "Men in Black" phenomenon has also been connected to them. These are the guys dressed in black suits, who intimidate many UFO researchers and abductees. Most appear to be government agents, but there are other expressions of them who do not look "human" in the usual sense.

They have a strange aura around them and, many people have reported, they can suddenly "disappear". I remember seeing a garage owner and UFO investigator telling his story on a TV program about Men in Black or "MIBs". They turned up out of nowhere without a vehicle and yet his garage was in the middle of the countryside, all by itself. After their conversation, they just as quickly vanished and it was impossible for them to do so under normal circumstances because you could see for miles in all directions.

The Men in Black are named after their dark clothing, mostly business or "agent" suits, and their dark glasses. This attire has all the signs of these beings needing protection from the Sun -a classic trait of the reptilians and greys. They are mostly described as having very white skin and, sometimes, olive skin. The texture is often said to be reptilian. Other strange traits in witness accounts are the trouble the MIBs appear to have breathing and the horrible smell, like sulphur, which abductees are constantly describing.

They also often arrive in "new" black cars that have not been manufactured for decades. Despite their apparent age, these vehicles show no signs of any wear or tear. It is as if they have just been driven from the factory. Similar beings, dressed in the context of the period, have been reported over the centuries in many parts of the world. The so-called Grim Reaper, who appeared in communities just before a lethal disease broke out, were described in terms that are remarkably close to today's Men in Black.

The Association of Extraterrestrial Investigations (APEX), founded by Dr. Max Berezowsky in Sao Paulo, Brazil, documented a Men in Black story involving a young guy called Aeromar[92].14 He said he was harassed by three men dressed in black suits and ties and he thought they were the police. He moved cities twice to get away from them and on one occasion complained to the police in Rio de Janeiro about their harassment.

They didn't believe him and he moved to Sao Paulo. It was there that a car stopped beside him in the street. He said he "lost his will to resist" and climbed inside to find the three guys who had been following him for months. He was driven to a wooden area, he said, where he saw a large "UFO". The car stopped and they all walked up to the craft, which was hovering above the ground and surrounded by a "luminous ring".

The next thing he knew, they were inside and he was sat in a chair with handles that secured his wrists. An iron bar pressed his head backwards against the chair and his neck was also fastened. Now, he said, the "Men in Black" transformed. Their "heads ripped open into a heart shape" and their skin became scaled and green like a reptilian.

This happened in 1979-80 long before MIBs became associated with reptilians. He said he also saw human corpses hanging from hooks. Everything went blank after that and he found himself back in the street where he was picked up. Now, however, it was hours later and there was no traffic. He ran home in a panic, he said, and told a roommate what had happened, but as he did so, a force threw him against a wall. The reptilians had told him never to talk about his experience. He was later introduced to Dr. Max Berezowsky and he told his story to APEX members.

On the superb US radio show, Sightings, a woman called Joyce Murphy talked about the reptilian shape-shifters of Brazil. She is the

---

92

president and founder of Beyond Boundaries, an organization that takes people on expeditions to many parts of the world. She was telling presenter Jeff Rense about some of the strange experiences on her travels when she talked about a policewoman she knew in Brazil who had described shape-shifting reptilian beings.

Joyce said:

"...she works in a very high position in the Sheriff's Office. There seem to be shapeshifters, here in Brazil at least, that try and get women to act as breeders for them. They actually shape-shifted to show them their actual form, a sort of reptilian type. This with her sister as a witness. And I know of another shape-shifter story.
    The daughter of an aviation engineer in Sao Paulo tells of a fellow student who revealed her true form changing...into a sort of reptilian being. These people do not know each other and they clam up if one goes after more information or wants to reveal the whole situation. Oh my gosh, what am I getting into here?"

The Reptilian Underground Bases
    There are so many reports of seeing reptilians and shape-shifting, but most people have no knowledge of this because 99% of the population gets their "news" and "information" from the mainstream media. The media, in turn, get their "news" and "information" overwhelmingly from official sources, which, like the media itself, are owned by the reptilian bloodlines. After speaking about the reptilians on the Sightings program, I was sent this account of an experience at the infamous Dulce underground facility in New Mexico.

These are the words of an army private employed on the surface:
    "...I was working on a routine job when another of the young enlistees, a mechanic, came in with a small rush job he wanted at once. He had the print and proceeded to show me exactly what he wanted. We are both bending over the bench in front of the welder when I happened to

look directly into his face. It seemed to suddenly become covered in a semi-transparent film or cloud. His features faded and in their place appeared a 'thing' with bulging eyes, no hair, and scales for skin."

He later saw the same thing happen to a guard at the Dulce front gate, and witnesses have spoken of seeing reptilian shape-shifters at the Madigan Military Hospital near Fort Lewis in Washington State. There are secret underground facilities throughout the world and at the deepest levels they open out into the inner-earth centers of the reptilians and greys.

Area 51 in Nevada is the best-known underground facility in UFO research circles, but the very fact that it is so famous and featured in Hollywood movies, shows that it is far from the most important of them. These facilities are themselves connected by a vast tunnel network that has been built with nuclear boring technology that the public never sees. It can cut tunnels at the rate of seven miles a day and these are an expansion of the global tunnel network created by the Atlanteans and Lemurians, and claimed by legends and accounts to exist under the United States, Central and South America, Britain, Egypt, Mesopotamia, Turkey, Asia, China, Malta, everywhere.

The tunnels have state-of-the-art transport systems that move at astonishing speeds. Insiders describe them as "magneto-leviton or mag-lev monorail trains capable of mach-2". Leading Illuminati companies and operations are involved in the construction. Companies like the Rand Corporation, General Electric, AT & T, Hughes Aircraft, Northrop Corporation, Sandia Corporation, Stanford Research Institute, Walsh Construction, the Colorado School of Mines, and the most significant one of all, Bechtel (Beck-tul), a major reptilian corporation.

These underground bases, tunnel systems, and their technology, have been detailed by former military personnel, mind-controlled slaves, and people like Phil Schneider, who helped to build some of them. Schneider was the son of a German U-boat commander in the Second World War, Otto Oscar Schneider. His father was captured and taken to the United States to work for the Illuminati.

As so often happens, the children of Illuminati operatives are brought up to work for the same masters and Phil Schneider says he was commissioned to build sections of a number of underground facilities in the United States. He said he knew of 131 underground military bases, an average of one mile deep, constructed for the New World Order agenda. Two of the bases he was involved with were Area 51 in Nevada and Dulce, New Mexico. Dulce is a small town of around 1,000 people and located on the Jicarilla Apache Reservation at a height of some 7,000 feet.

From in and around Dulce have come a stream of reports of UFO sightings and landings, "alien" abductions, human and animal mutilations, and sightings of reptilians. The base was also the alleged scene, in 1979, of the "Dulce Wars" when reptilians and greys are said to have battled with human military and civilian personnel. Many people on both sides were killed and Phil Schneider claims to have taken part in this shoot-out. He said he was hit by a laser weapon and he had a fantastic scar down his chest, as he publicly revealed.

Schneider talked of his part in the battle in a lecture in 1995, although there appear to be many other elements to it, also:

"My job was to go down the holes and check the rock samples, and recommend the explosive to deal with the particular rock. As I was headed down there, we found ourselves amidst a large cavern that was full of outer-space aliens, otherwise known as large Greys. I shot two of them. At that time, there were 30 people down there. About 40 more came down after this started, and all of them got killed. We had surprised a whole underground base of existing aliens. Later, we found out that they had been living on our planet for a long time. ...This could explain a lot of what is behind the theory of ancient astronauts."

Schneider began to speak out and alert the world to what was going on, although as usual most people didn't listen. Schneider, who worked closely with researcher Alex Christopher, died in January 1996 in highly suspicious circumstances that were crudely made to look like suicide.

Schneider, speaking at a public lecture a year earlier, said:

"...for every calendar year that transpires, military technology increases about 44.5 years [compared with the increase rate of 'conventional' technology]. This is why it is easy to understand that back in 1943 they were able to create, through the use of vacuum tube technology, a ship that could literally disappear from one place and appear in another place."

This was a reference to the "Philadelphia Experiment" in which a US naval ship is alleged to have been made invisible and taken into another dimension. Another of the underground bases Schneider helped to build is under the new Denver International Airport, east of Denver. The construction was very controversial because of the massive cost overrun - the same as the gigantic hole being dug by Bechtel as part of "transport improvements" in Boston, Massachusetts.

Denver Airport is the place with the gargoyles, Freemasonic symbols, and murals full of Illuminati symbolism. I have been through there myself a number of times. According to Schneider, there are several main levels underneath, at least ten sublevels, a 4.5-square-mile underground city, and an 88.5-square-mile underground base. The Denver base is said to include massive "containment camps" and fenced in areas deep underground for holding "dissidents".

Workers who experienced the deeper levels of the base saw scenes so terrifying they have refused to talk about them. From other sources, however, we can imagine some of what they saw. These bases are where many of the millions, yes millions, of children who go missing every year worldwide are taken. 1 know it is hard to stomach, but they are used for slave labor and eaten by the reptilians, just like humans eat chicken or cows.

Workers at the Dulce base in New Mexico have reported seeing the most grotesque sights in the lower levels. Researchers Bill Hamilton and TAL Levesque (also known as Jason Bishop III) gathered the following information about Dulce, which they published in UFO magazine:

"Level number six is privately called 'Nightmare Hall'. It holds the Genetic Labs. Reports from workers who have seen bizarre experimentation are as follows: 'I have seen multi-legged "humans" that look like half-human/half octopus. Also reptilian-humans and furry creatures that have hands like humans and cry like a baby. It mimics human words...also a huge mixture of lizard-humans in cages. There are fish, seals, birds and mice that can hardly be considered those species. There are several cages (and vats) of winged humanoids, grotesque bat-like creatures...but three and a half to seven feet tall. Gargoyle-like beings and Draco reptoids.

"Level number seven is worse, row after row of thousands of humans and human mixtures in cold storage. Here, too, are embryo storage vats of humanoids in various stages of development. [One worker said] '...I frequently encountered humans in cages; usually dazed or drugged, but sometimes they cried and begged for help. We were told they were hopelessly insane, and involved in high-risk drug tests to cure insanity. We were told never to try to speak to them at all. At the beginning we believed that story. Finally, in 1978, a small group of workers discovered the truth'..."

This discovery led to the "Dulce Wars", the battle between humans and the reptilians and reptilian greys in 1979 when many scientists and military personnel were killed, and Phil Schneider says he was critically wounded.

A security officer at Dulce called Thomas Castello has described to researchers what happens at the Dulce base and his words were reported in the UFO magazine article. His information has also been circulated as the "Dulce Papers". Castello worked for seven years with the Rand Corporation, an Illuminati operation in Santa Monica, California, and transferred to Duke in 1977.

He estimated there were more than 18,000 of the "short greys" at Dulce, and he had also seen tall reptilian humanoids. He knew of seven levels, but there could have been more, and he said the "aliens" were on levels five, six, and seven. The lower you go, the higher the security clearance you need. The only sign in English was above the tube shuttle station which said "to Los Alamos", another major underground reptilian base in New Mexico. Most signs at Dulce are in the "alien symbol language" and a universal symbol system understood by humans and aliens, he said.

The Illuminati communicate above ground in the language of symbolism, as revealed in The Biggest Secret and the Symbolism Archive on my website. The hieroglyphics of Sumer, Egypt, and China, would have been a reptilian or "alien" language originally. Other tunnel connections from Dulce went to underground facilities at Page, Arizona, Area 51 in Nevada, Taos, Carlsbad, and Datil, New Mexico, Colorado Springs and Creede, Colorado. Castello said there was a vast network of tube shuttle connections under the United States, which extends into a global system of tunnels and sub-cities.

He described the immense security at Dulce. Below the second level, everyone is weighed naked and given a uniform. Any change in weight is noted and people are examined and X-rayed if there is a change of three pounds.

At the entrance to all "sensitive" areas there are scales and a person's weight must match with their card and code to gain entry. Castello also revealed some of the genetic work carried out at Dulce. He said that their scientists can separate the "bioplasmic body" from the physical body and place an "alien entity" (consciousness) within a human body after removing the "soul" of the human. I have thought for years that some famous people, including prime ministers and presidents, were taken into such facilities and possessed by a reptilian entity.

To the public the famous person looks the same physically afterwards, but now a very different force is deciding the behavior. Ancient legends also tell of people being replaced in the night by "changelings" or shape-shifters. It is likely that certain bloodlines with a threshold ratio of reptilian DNA makes this possession easier and this is one reason why the Illuminati keep such detailed genetic records of family bloodlines.

The joint global press announcement by the Illuminati's Bill Clinton and Tony Blair in 2000 about the mapping of the human genome takes on even greater significance when you think that the US Department of Energy has laboratories at Dulce and is closely connected to the genome project, along with the National Institute of Health, the National Science Foundation, and the Howard Hughes Medical Institute. All are Illuminati fronts.

Researcher Alan Walton, who writes extensively on the Internet about the reptilian connection, says:

"Underneath most major cities, especially in the USA in fact, there exist subterranean counterpart 'cities' controlled by the Masonic/hybrid/alien 'elite'. Often surface/ subsurface terminals exist beneath Masonic Lodges, police stations, airports, and federal buildings of major cities ... and even not so 'major' cities. The population ratio is probably close to 10% of the population (the hybrid military-industrial fraternity 'elite' living below ground as opposed to the 90% living above). This does not include the full-blood reptilian species that live in even deeper recesses of the Earth.

"Some of the major population centers were deliberately established by the Masonic/hybrid elite of the Old and New 'worlds' to afford easy access to already existing underground levels, some of which are thousands of years old. Considering that the Los Alamos Labs [in New Mexico] had a working prototype nuclear powered thermal-bore drill that could literally melt tunnels through the Earth at a rate of 8 mph 40 years ago, you can imagine how extensive these underground systems have become.

These sub-cities also offer close access to organized criminal syndicates, which operate on the surface. They have developed a whole science of 'borgonomics' through which they literally nickel-and-dime us into slavery via multi-leveled taxation, inflation, sublimation, manipulation, regulation, fines, fees, licenses... and the entire debt-credit scam which is run by the Federal Reserve and Wall Street.

"New York City, I can confirm, is one of the largest draconian nests in the world. Or rather the ancient underground 'Atlantean' systems that network beneath that area. They literally control the entire Wall Street pyramid from below... with more than a little help from reptilian bloodlines like the Rockefellers, etc. In fact these reptilian genetic lines operate in a parasitic manner, the underground society acting as the 'parasite' society and the surface society operating as the 'host' society. ...As for the New York City / Wall Street 'nest', during the bombing of the World Trade Center (aka World Slave Center) wherein terrorists attempted to topple one of the towers into the other, a little known fact was briefly revealed.

A six-leveled sub-basement controlled by the US Secret Service suffered heavy damage. These six sub-basements, one beneath the other, may not have ended there, based on other information that I've uncovered of massive alien infestation beneath the New York City area. These subbasements may actually serve as a major terminal between the underground society of Masonic elite, and the surface society which it controls."

I am sure that the locations of these major cities were selected because they were above underground reptilian-Nephilim tunnel and cavern systems and/or they were on significant vortex points. Phoenix, Arizona, is built on one of these ancient networks, as is Los Angeles -the city of the "angels".

Lauren Savage, the Webmaster of http://www.davidicke.com in Texas, says that every county in that state has a building with gothic European architecture (i.e. reptilian), which could not normally have been afforded by Texas when these settlements were built in the 1870's. Many have gargoyles. These buildings, he says, are the county courthouses sitting above underground tunnels and basement systems.

Dallas is an example with its underground tunnels beneath Dealey Plaza where President Kennedy was shot in 1963. What a great way for the true assassins to escape. These tunnels would have been under the original Masonic lodge in Dallas, which was located in Dealey Plaza.

Close by is the 1870's old red courthouse complete with gargoyles. Underground tunnels were discovered in Dallas in the late 50's or early 60's and Lauren talked to a man who was working on a state road crew when he was a teenager.

They were digging out what is called "the canyon" to build freeways when they opened up an ancient tunnel. They found rail-type tracks and a sort of train with no known source of fuel or energy. They followed the tunnel to where it ended or collapsed, under an old livery stable. Dallas was a French settlement, earlier called Arcadia (an Illuminati code relating to Atlantis), and a suburb is still named Arcadia Park. In 1999, they revealed that the Capitol building in Austin has underground facilities, which they were going to restore. This building was the headquarters of George W. Bush before he was manipulated into the presidency.

Alan Walton says that Thomas Castello, the Dulce security director, described how the greys, "reptiloids", and winged "mothmen" collaborate in the lower levels of the underground system, which includes Dulce and Los Alamos. The command pyramid, he says, seems to be mothmen, reptiloids, and greys, with the hybrids and humans under them.

Castello also says that one of the reptiloids told him that the surface of the Earth was their original home before they were removed in a war the war of the gods -in far ancient times. They escaped underground, to other stars and planets, and even into the fourth and fifth dimensions, Castello says he was told. This fits with the accounts of Credo Mutwa and many abductees who have told of how the reptilians evolved on this planet and were overpowered by other extraterrestrial groups, especially the Nordics.

A woman known as "D" claims to have seen the underground facilities at China Lake Naval Weapons Centre in the California Desert, one of the major mind control centers of North America.18 It straddles a vast area and very little can be seen above ground. I have driven around the outside of the base twice now. On one side the public road runs alongside the perimeter fence for a while.

The entrance to China Lake is in the little town of Ridgecrest and this is where "D" once lived. Ridgecrest is home to many mind-controlled slaves programmed at China Lake and it's not far from where the mass murderer Charles Manson and his "Family" used to live. "D", a victim of trauma-based mind control, said that the military chose her because of her bloodline. They had told her that before the development of language, humans communicated by telepathy thanks to a hormone secreted in the brain.

This hormone, she was told, was no longer operating in most people, only in particular bloodlines, including hers, and they wanted to use these abilities. The period, thousands of years ago, when this telepathic human brain function was genetically suppressed was almost certainly symbolized by the story common to most ancient cultures of the gods giving people different languages to divide them and stop them communicating.

"D" said she was taken underground at China Lake and saw the genetics laboratory and holding center for captured humans and genetically engineered mutants. (The true symbolism of the Mutant Ninja Turtles who lived underground in "sewer" tunnels and came out to "fight evil"?) Reptilian symbolism, most of it painting reptilians in a very positive light, has been bombarding the minds of children in recent years.

"D" described seeing horrendous creatures of all types, shapes, and sizes at China Lake. She said she was shown these horrors to let her see what would happen to her if she did not co-operate and she claimed her own son had been murdered. Under China Lake, she said, a reptilian sexually assaulted her and she saw another cut open the chest of a grey. "D" confirmed from her experience that the greys are terrified of the reptilian leadership and do whatever they tell them.

On another occasion, she said, she was taken to the reptilian base under the appropriately named Death Valley, a relatively short drive from China Lake. There she said she saw a reptilian leader, much taller than the others, who was wearing an Egyptian headdress with a cobra snake motif.

The respected UFO researcher, Timothy Good, quotes two "high-placed sources" in his book, Unearthly Disclosure, who confirm the existence of underground extraterrestrial bases. One was from the US Air Force and the other from the US Navy. The reliability of these sources was supported by Admiral of the Fleet, Lord Hill-Norton, the former chief of the UK Defense Staff and former chairman of the NATO Military Committee.

Good says that the sources provided evidence that the American military was working with unidentified "aliens" who have established bases on the planet.19' Many of these bases were underwater, Good was told, a fact that would fit with the ancient legends of the "gods" emerging from the water. The sources said that bases exist in Australia, the Pacific Ocean, the former Soviet Union, the United States, and the Caribbean.

The latter is believed to be in Puerto Rico. The US air force contact told Good: "They [the "aliens"] are here on a permanent basis. They are after this planet." He also said they were "messing with plate tectonics", the movement of land that causes earthquakes, and that the warming of the world's oceans was connected to extraterrestrial activity20 Well it isn't global warming, that's for sure.

Interestingly, Good's sources suggested that the "aliens" were involved in "hybridization" experiments to allow their race to take over the planet... This, however, began a long, long, time ago.

T'was always so

The stories of reptilians and other non-human races living within the Earth in what we would today call "bases", cities, or tunnel networks, can be found widely described in ancient accounts also. The Nagas, or serpent people, in India and throughout Asia and the Far East, were said to live in two main underground centers called Patala and Bhogavati.

From there, according to Hindu legend, they battle for power with the Nordic underground kingdoms of Agharta and Shambala. Hindus believe that Patala can be entered at the Well of Sheshna in Benares, while Bhogavati is believed to be in the Himalayas. Similar stories of underground caverns and tunnel systems can be found in Tibet and China. In the Gilgamesh stories of the Sumerian tablets, we are told of vast underground cities.

Gilgamesh was a "demi-god" and "semi-divine" (reptilian hybrid) who sought the immortality of the "gods". The stories speak of KI-GAL or "the Great Below", which was ruled by the goddess Ereshkigal and the god Mergal. In the KI-GAL were violent guardians called "scorpion men", reanimated human bodies, spirits and the "undead", and robotic beings known as Galatur or Gala, which were used to abduct humans from the surface.

There were "eagle-headed" reptilians, which were often said to have wings. The accounts describe a race called the Pazazu, a dog-faced "human" with reptilian scales and tail. All this sounds remarkably like the scenes described at Dulce today. Chinese legend claims that an underground world entered from the Eastern Mountain of Taishan was guarded by vicious demons called Men Shen with animal-like faces or masks.

This was the Chinese "Hell" and it is said that the Lords of Hell interacted with the Dragon Kings on the surface. The Japanese "Hell" or underground network was similar, and among the non-human entities were the Kappa, semi-aquatic reptilian humanoids and other shape-shifters who lived in mountains, under the ground, or under the sea.

In Viking-Norse legend they have the giant serpent, Nidhoggr or Jormungand, that lived underground and this was similar to the giant serpent Apophis in Egyptian myth. The Scandinavians and Germans had their Huldre or "Hidden Folk" who were also known as the elves. One of the codes for the bloodline is "elven" and the beings of folklore like trolls, etins, fairies, elves, troglodytes, Nephilim, Brownies or Braunies, and the "little people" of Ireland are all different names for the subterranean entities described in the modern accounts of "ET bases".21

All the same stories are associated with them -interbreeding with humans, unable to go out in the sunlight, and all the rest. They even mention the "missing time" experience of people abducted by the "fairies" and include many stories of these underground folk killing and mutilating cattle and taking the blood. Michael Mott has produced an excellent collection of these stories on underground dwellers in folklore and myth.

His book is called Caverns, Cauldrons, And Concealed Creatures, and is available through my website. He writes that England, Scotland, Wales, and Ireland all have endless traditions of underground peoples with many similarities and common origins between them. It seems to me that Scotland, Ireland, and the British Isles in general are such a major center for the Illuminati bloodlines because of the number of entrances to the underground world there are in that region. It is the same with other parts of the world like France, Germany, and the Caucasus Mountains.

What is really under the Windsors' Balmoral Castle or the Queen Mother's Glamis Castle in Scotland, that key country for Illuminati bloodlines? Interestingly, there is a legendary "secret room" at Glamis. According to a guest, the writer, Sir Walter Scott, and others, it is the family's law or custom that the secret is known to only three people at one time.

They take a "terrible oath" not to reveal the secret. Another guest, Lord Halifax, said that in 1875 a workman at the castle came across a door leading to a long passageway. The man investigated, but then he saw something that made him run back in terror. When the 13th Earl of Strathmore was told what the workman had seen he persuaded him to accept money to emigrate and give his word never to reveal what he saw. Lord Halifax said that after the incident the Earl was a changed man, who became silent and moody, with an "anxious, scared face".

The Norse/Germanic fairies, goblins, trows, knockers, brownies, leprechauns, sidhe (shee), tylwyth teg (terlooeth teig) and so on were either malevolent or indifferent to humanity, Michael Mott says. They lived, virtually without exception, under the ground. Mounds, hills, ruins, ancient raths or hill-forts, mountains, cliffs, and ancient cities were said to be the "rooftops" of their palaces.

Beings that mirror modern reports of the Sasquatch (Big Foot) and the Yeti (Abominable Snowman) can also be found in ancient stories of underground creatures that come to the surface. Like the Nagas, the serpent people of Asia, European folklore often claimed that these "fairy" people entered their underground homes through lakes.

Michael Mott continues:

"To remove all doubt as to their relationship with Norse hidden-folk and Indian Nagas alike, they shunned the sunlight, and often seemed interested in crossbreeding their own bloodlines with those of human beings, or even in crossbreeding their 'livestock' or fairy cattle, horses, hounds and so forth with the surface species which were most compatible. The goblin-dwarf, Rumplestiltskin, in his lust to have the human baby and its genetic bounty, is just one example of this in folklore.

The elves took a regular interest in human affairs-weddings, births, and deaths, (bloodlines), the success of crops and livestock, and so forth - but only for their own selfish interests. They seemed to be overly-concerned with genetic and biological diversity, and they pilfered livestock, crops, and human genes via theft or cross-species liaison whenever they saw fit to do so. The elves are generally depicted as extremely fair-haired and fair-skinned."22

What Mott is describing there from European folklore could have come straight from the mouth of a modern abductee or researcher of the underground bases. The so-called greys of modern UFO legend appear to be the same as the beings known as the Galatur and Ushabtiu who abducted humans from underground in Sumerian and Egyptian myths, and the folklore of the Shetland Islands off the north of Scotland referred to the "little men" who abducted humans as "grey neighbors" and the greys.

In the Americas you find the same legends and accounts of the underground people. They include humans, reptilians, reptilian humanoids, and various "monsters" and "demons". Their descriptions match those of other ancient cultures all over the world. Many Native American tribes, like the Hopi, claim to have lived within these underground cavern "cities" before coming to settle on the surface.

In the Mayan epic, the Popol Vuh, two "semi-divine" (hybrid) brothers, Hunapuh and Xbalanque, enter the horrific underground world called Xibalba to battle a crocodile-headed monster and, as a result of their victory, the brothers brought an end to human sacrifice -the calling card of the reptilians to this day. These underground worlds are the origin of the belief in Hell being under the Earth. The poet, Dante (1265-1321), was an initiate of the Knights Templar. In his famous work, the Inferno, he is taken on a tour of the underworld. He says it consisted of ten levels where "sinners" are imprisoned and punished by horned demons and reptilian, bird-like giants called the harpies.

The conditions and environment he describes in this "Hell" can be found in descriptions of these underground worlds and cavern communities everywhere. The accounts even include the idea of being imprisoned down there waiting for the day of judgment.

In Ireland and the Isle of Man, two major locations for Illuminati bloodlines and activity, much of their culture is based on fairy legends and "the little people" who live under the ground. Irish legends tell of the sexual relationships between the ancient Milesians and the Tuatha de Danaan, the Irish "underground gods" who fled into the Earth and settled there. St Patrick, who "removed the snakes from Ireland", is said to have seen one of these underground people, a "fairy woman", coming out of the cave of Cruachan.

When St Patrick asks a Milesian about her, he replies:

"She is of the Tuatha de Danaan who are unfading...and I am of the sons of Mil [human Irish], who are perishable and fade away."

The usual tale of mortality and immortality. As Michael Mott reports, Daniel Bradley and other geneticists at the Trinity College in Dublin have discovered that the oldest "pure" racial bloodline in Europe continues to exist in the far west of Ireland.

This, as I highlight in The Biggest Secret, is also the last bastion of an ancient Irish language called Gaelic, which is astonishingly similar to languages of North Africa, such as Libyan. Bradley told the Reuters news agency in March 2000 that the Irish came from a race that was different to other Europeans. He said: "When you look at this old genetic geography of Ireland what you find is that in the west (of Ireland) we are almost exclusively of one type of Y chromosome."

They found that 98% of men with Gaelic names in western Ireland had this particular chromosome. If anyone is still in doubt that the legends of the "fairy" people and the "extraterrestrial" accounts of today are describing the same entities, Michael Mott summarizes here the common attributes of the underground peoples of global folklore:

"They are mostly reptilian or reptilian humanoids or "fair" and Nordic; they are telepathic with superior mental powers; they can shape-shift and create illusions; they want to interbreed with humans and need human blood, flesh, and reproductive materials; they have advanced technology; they have the secret of immortality; they can fly, either by themselves or with their technology; they mostly have a malevolent agenda for humans; they cannot survive for long in direct sunlight; they have been banished from the surface world or are in hiding from surface people and/or the Sun; they want to keep their treasures, knowledge, and true identity a secret; they covertly manipulate events on the surface world; they have surface humans working for them through the priesthoods, cults, and secret societies; they have a putrid smell like "sulphur and brimstone".

The accounts are incredibly consistent over thousands of years.

Mott writes:

"The reptilian aspect of some underworlders permeates folklore. One universal theme that recurs in the folktales of many, many cultures is that of the snake-husband or snake-wife, who can transform into a "human" or humanoid form and is invariably (of course) of royal blood among his or her own kind (talk about the ultimate pick-up line!). Often the snake or serpent-man exacts a promise of marriage, or the hand of an unborn human child in betrothal, consistent with the theme of the subterranean's interest in maintaining their own genetic diversity.

"A variant of this should be familiar to most readers of fairy tales, in the form of 'The Frog Prince'. The frog-prince is a Handsome Prince, but like the Japanese seducing dragon, he has a reptilian or amphibian form. The underworld link is complete, for frequently the frog lives in a deep well, from which he is discovered or rescued by the female protagonist.

A possible connection is evident in the Scandinavian belief that some dwarves would 'turn into toads", if caught by the Sun, much like Mimoto's lover turned from a man into a 'dragon' when the same thing happened. Slovenia has its legends of fairies and 'little people', but Slovenian fairy tales are also permeated by the presence of the 'Snake Queen', a great, white, cave-dwelling creature who is part woman and part serpent. The serpentine-yet-human Nagas are still believed by devout Hindus and some Buddhists to dwell beneath India, Nepal, and Tibet."23

Denying The Obvious

When you read and hear the horrendous accounts of the victims and witnesses of the grotesque reptilian agenda, ancient and modern, it is hard to comprehend how so many "researchers" and New Agers continue to believe that this "extraterrestrial" presence is good for humanity and a sign of positive change. Now, of course, not all "extraterrestrials" or interdimensionals are malevolent, but does that mean that we have to ignore the fact that some of them are?

I have had "researchers" attack me who appear far more concerned with the effect of my work on the image of reptilians than they are with the horrors being perpetrated on abductees, mind-control victims, and the people of the world in general.

Dr. David Jacobs in his book, The Threat, picks up this point. He calls such people "the Positives":

"Often the New Age Positives band together into almost cult-like groups to defend themselves from their detractors -researchers and abductees who have come to different conclusions about the abduction phenomenon. The Positives reinforce one another's feelings and insulate themselves from the terror of their lives; they become angry when "less enlightened" abduction researchers question their interpretation."

Certain researchers in England, Las Vegas, and the United States in general come immediately to mind. Dr. Jacobs also names some of the "stars" of extraterrestrial research like John Hunter Gray, Dr. Leo Sprinkle, Dr. Richard Boylan, Joseph Nyman, and Harvard professor, Dr. John Mack, among those who want to put a positive twist on the abductee reports:

"Both Boylan and Mack de-emphasize the effects of the standard abduction procedures. Boylan believes that gynecological and urological procedures take place only with a very small number of abductees and he rarely focuses on them. And although Mack has found nearly the full range of alien physical, mental, and reproductive procedures, he only mentions them in passing while emphasizing what he finds to be spiritually uplifting elements.

The benevolent 'spin' that the Positives (both abductees and researchers) put on the abduction phenomenon is puzzling, given the way most people describe their abductions: being unwillingly taken; being subjected to painful physical procedures (sometimes leaving permanent scars); enduring humiliating and abusive sexual episodes, including unwanted sexual intercourse; living with the fear and anxiety of wondering when they will be abducted again."[25]

James Bartley, the abductee and researcher of the reptilian connection, is rather more blunt in his appraisal of what he calls "the Muppets" -those who either refuse to see the malevolent nature of the reptilian agenda or actively seek to portray it in a positive light. He says the reason why so many abductees are hopelessly confused about this whole mess is because trigger mechanisms have been programmed into them to keep them from getting at the truth of their experiences.

He says he has witnessed countless times how an abductee will immediately fall asleep the moment the lecturer begins talking about "fear-based" issues. But when he or she attends a lecture by a channeller or some other "light worker" saying positive things about the "aliens", the abductee is bright and attentive, and awake during the whole lecture.

"Falling asleep is just one trigger mechanism," he says.

Another is annoyance or anger at the "fear-based" lecturer or abductee. Likewise an overwhelming compulsion to get up and walk out, to get up and eat, to get up and smoke a cigarette, getting nauseous, a headache etc., etc. In an article challenging the methods of researcher and lecturer, Dr. Richard Boylan, Bartley goes on:

"Boylan... [promotes]... the ludicrous notion that a woman abductee was merely suffering from spiritual retardation and was mentally incapable of understanding the 'benevolent' nature of the horrific and unwanted experimentation that was being conducted on her...We have worked with countless women who have suffered painful and bloody hemorrhages, sometimes lasting for days, after the 'benevolent ET' doctors had made an unwanted house call.

What, the discerning human must ask, does profuse and painful bleeding have to do with 'spiritual' evolution? The New Age La-Dee-Dahs claim that there is no such thing as Evil or Demons, which makes [them] the butt of endless jokes by Witches, Warlocks and Satanists throughout the world because the latter derive their power from demonic entities.

"By constantly blaming 'the military' and the 'globalist industrialists', the reptilian propagandists condition the abductees into believing that all human institutions are bad and that the only hope one has to reach the... 'next level of consciousness, evolution, vibratory frequency' et al, is to look to the skies towards the same dark gods who are responsible for their current state of spiritual enslavement.

Never mind that for the most part these 'Globalists and Militarists' are part of the same old fraternal orders, which worship the patriarchal serpent gods and in many cases are hosts for reptilian entities themselves. These hosts and their fellow travelers operate as a Fifth Column here on Earth to set the stage for the return of the Dark Reptilian Gods.

"The so-called UFO Research Community is awash with these 'Muppets'. Even I have to laugh at the irony of it: literal hosts for reptilian entities facilitating abductee support groups, lecturing at so-called 'UFO Conferences' and speaking on the Art-Bell Show [the major "mysteries" radio show in the US]. This is so because of the long term genetic and soul matrix manipulation of the human race."26

How right he is and how fast the human race needs to wake up and grow up. The stories I have featured in this chapter are just a small selection of the reports and personal accounts describing reptilian experiences. If you want to see more, go to the Reptilian Archive on my website, read The Biggest Secret, or watch the Bridge of Love videos with Arizona Wilder, Revelations Of A Mother Goddess, and Credo Mutwa, The Reptilian Agenda, parts one and two.

When you put these modern reports together with their mirrors in the ancient world, it constitutes a library of information that only the most imprisoned of minds could dismiss without further investigation.

But, given the level of human conditioning, many still will. Especially the media.

CHAPTER THIRTEEN
THE WRAP-UP

Now you may be wondering why, if there has been, and is, a super-secret, powerful secret society operating in the background why they have not achieved their goal of total domination of the human race. It is a good question and one that has a very good answer. There seems to exist an equally powerful secret society with the goal of assuring that there is not total world domination by this secret society. However, the discussion of this opposing force will be left for another day. Sufficite it for now that we have proven that there exists a number of secret societies that work from the shadows in order to manipulate mankind.

Now it is up to the reader to look for and understand the machinations of these secret societies as they work to carry out their nefarious deeds. Are they working for our good, or to further the desires of those mysterious beings that lurk in the shadows?

INDEX

A

Abductions, 25, 65
Adapa, 28, 106
Agharta, 36, 37, 189
AGLA, 149, 150, 152, 159, 162
Allen, Gary, 62, 66, 70, 84
Andrews, George, 49
Angel, 22
Angel of Death, 4
Annunaki, 26, 28, 31, 32, 33, 96, 106, 108, 109
Anshar, 26, 32
Anu, 26, 28, 32, 105, 106
Anunnakku, 32
Aryans, 41, 102, 164
Association of Extraterrestrial Investigations, 57, 178
Association of Helpers, 144, 145
Astral projection, 134
Atlantis, 36, 43, 187
Auschwitz, 77, 83, 84
Axelrod, Alan, 12
Ayurveda, 133

B

Babylon-Working, 96
Barrett, David V., 12
Benevolent Ones, 23
Berossus, 27
Black Knights of the Thule Society, 39
Black Sun, 39, 40, 41, 44, 123
Black, Edwin, 84
Black, Jeremy, 32
Britain, 62
Brotherhood of the Snake, 104, 108
Brothers of the Light Society, 39
Bulwer-Lytton, Edward, 39
Bush, George H.W., President, 42
Bush, George Herbert Walker President, 63

C

CA, Deep Springs,, 50
Cabalistic Jews, 66
Cagliostro, Count, 66, 67
Cargo cults, 14
Cathars, 119
Catholic Church, 66
CFR, 42, 63
Charlemagne the Great, 114
Chinese medicine, 134
Church of Scotland, 112
CIA, 49, 50, 89, 92, 93, 94
Clark's Law, 14, 137

'Commander X', 47

C

Communist Manifesto, 70, 85
Communist Movement, 64
Compagnie de St Sacrement, 155
Company of the Most Blessed Sacrament, 156
Continuity of Operations Plan, 90
Cooper, Milton William, 26
Council on Foreign Relations, 42, 62, 63, 64, 66, 145
Cromwell, Oliver, 71, 72

D

Demon, 22
Denver Airport, 182
Diamond Syndicate., 140
Disinformation, 24
Disraeli, Benjamin, 44

Divine Right of Kings', 110
Divine Ships, 103
Drug trade, 26
Dugway Proving Ground, 50
Dulce Wars, 181, 183

E

Ea, 28, 32, 105, 106, 107, 108
Egypt, 36, 43, 103, 108, 115, 116, 118, 126, 180, 184
Egyptian Book of the Dead, 103
Elder Race, 36, 41
Enki, 28
Epic of Creation, 32

F

F.B.I., 61
Fisher King, 123
Fish-Goat-Man, 119
Founding Fathers, 62
French Revolution, 69

G

Garden of Eden, 46, 106, 165
General of the Society, 144
Georgia Guide Stones, 95
Golden Dawn, 62
Goring, Hermann, 40
Grail Bloodline, 114, 117, 119
Grail Stone', 122
Grand Master, 103, 166
Great Seal of the United States, 85
Green, Anthony, 32

H

HAARP, 96
Hamilton, Bill, 182
Haushofer, Karl, 39
Helvetius, 33, 34, 35
Hidden One, 118

Himmler, Heinrich, 40, 83
Hitler, Adolf, 40, 64, 74, 75
Holy Bible, 19
Holy Grail, 97, 114, 120
Hudnall, Ken, 14, 17

I

Igigi, 31, 32
Illuminati, 66, 69, 70, 85
Invisible Government, 89, 90, 92, 93, 95

J

Jacobs, David Dr., 163, 195
Jefferson, Thomas, 84, 85
Jenseitsflugmaschine, 41
Jesuit, 66
Jesuits, 66

K

Keel, John A., 45
Ken Hudnall Show, 130
Kennedy, John, 25, 26
Ki, 26, 32
Kimberley, 140
King James VI, 109
King of the World, 119, 120, 121, 122, 124
Kishar, 26, 32
Knights Templar, 44, 66, 193
Kronos, 117, 118, 123, 124, 127

L

Last Will and Testament of Cecil Rhodes, 43
Le Roi du Monde, 118, 125
League of Just Men, 70
Leigh, Richard, 66, 69
Lenin, 64
Levesque, TAL, 182
Library of Ashurbanipal, 28
Lodge of the Nine Muses, 85
Lord of the Earth, 119, 120, 122, 123, 125

Lord of the Mountain, 123
Lord Yahweh, 115
Lords of the Black Stone, 39
Lords of the Inner Earth, 41

M

Marduk, 32
Marx, Karl, 70
Masons, 62
Master Race, 75
Masters, 66, 75
Men In Black, 48, 50, 51, 57, 75, 177
Mengele, Josef, 77, 83
Merchant Bankers, 65
Merovingian Bloodline, 114
Michael, 66, 69
MJ-12, 26
Montauk Project, 96
Morell, Theodor Dr., 41
Mount Lassen, 170
Mount Weather, 91

N

N M Rothschild & Sons, 140
Napoleon, 64, 72
National Security Council, 89, 92
New Mexico, Dulce, 47, 50, 181
New World Order, 42, 43, 44, 95, 181
NSA, 49

O

Oannes, 27, 28
Old Ones, 36
Oliver, Revilo P. Professor, 12
OMEGA Group, 46
Omega Press, 3
One world government., 63, 66
Order of Melchizedek, 121
Order of Skull and Bones, 42
Order of the Bees, 85
Orsic, Maria, 41

P

Persia, 36, 126
Philadelphia Experiment, 96, 97, 182
Philip the Fair of France, 66
Pinkham, Mark Amaru, 169
Pioneer Fruit Growing Company, 140
Presence, 23, 24, 25
Prester John, 122
Prince of Earth, 107

Q

Quigley, Carroll Historian, 144

R

Rama, 15
Reagan, Ronald President, 43, 63
Rennes-le-Château, 151, 158
Report from Iron Mountain, 95
Reptilians, 104, 165
Rhodes Fruit Farms, 140, 141
Rhodes, Cecil, 63, 139, 140, 141, 142, 144
Rhodesia, 63
Rhone and Boschendal, 141
Rig Veda, 15
Robertson, Pat, 42
Rothschild, 65, 66, 67
Round Table Group, 42, 143, 145, 146
Round Table Groups, 66
Round Table Journal, 143
Round Table movement, 143
Royal Institute of International Affairs, 64, 145
Rugen, 42
Rund flugzeug, 42
Russian Revolution, 64, 65

S

Satan, 67
Saunière, 151, 152, 153, 161, 162
Schiff, Jacob, 64

Schulmann, W. O., 41
Secret Societies, 25, 61, 63, 66, 69
Serpent People, 36, 45, 46, 47
Shadow People', 130
Shepherd Kings, 118
Sitchin, Zacharia, 27, 105, 106
Sitchin, Zecharia, 19
Situation Room, 93
Snake Marsh, 106
Society of the Elect, 144, 145, 146
Space Brothers, 23
Special Group, 92, 93
Stanford Research Institute, 88, 180
Sumerian Civilization, 19

T

Tavistock, 88
Technical University of Munich, 41
Templars, 66
Temple of Solomon, 103
Temple University, 163
Texas
    El Paso, 3, 4
The Earth Chronicles, 105

'

'The Moot', 146

T

The Round Table, 64
The Threat: The Secret Agenda, 163

Third Reich, 75
Thule Sonnenrad, 40
Time dilation, 135
Time travel, 41, 97, 135
Titans, 36, 37
Trew Law of Free Monarchies, 113
Trilateral Commission, 42, 64
Trotsky, 64

U

Uanna, 28
UFO, 18, 21, 22, 25, 67, 75
UFOs, 18, 20, 22, 65
United Nations, 61
United States, 64, 65, 84
Utah, Dugway, 50

V

Vril Gesellschaft, 41
Vril Lodge, 40
Vril Society, 39, 41

W

Walden, James L., 165
Wang. Connie, 4
War of 1812, 90
Washington D.C, 61
Washington, George, 166
Weishaupt, Adam, 66, 67, 70
World War II, 75

www.ingramcontent.com/pod-product-compliance
Lightning Source LLC
Chambersburg PA
CBHW050841040426
42333CB00058B/210